Dear Reader:

The book you are about to read is the latest bestseller from St. Martin's True Crime Library, the imprint *The New York Times* calls "the leader in true crime!" Each month, we offer you a fascinating account of the latest, most sensational crime that has captured national attention. *The Milwaukee Murders* delves into the twisted world of Jeffrey Dahmer, one of the most savage serial killers of our time; *Lethal Lolita* gives you the *real* scoop on the deadly love affair between Amy Fisher and Joey Buttafuoco; *Whoever Fights Monsters* takes you inside the special FBI team that tracks serial killers; *Garden of Graves* reveals how police uncovered the bloody human harvest of mass murderer Joel Rifkin; *Unanswered Cries* is the story of a detective who tracked a killer for a year, only to discover it was someone he knew and trusted; *Bad Blood* is the story of the notorious Menendez brothers and their sensational trials; *Sins of the Mother* details the sad account of Susan Smith and her two drowned children; *Fallen Hero* details the riveting tragedy of O. J. Simpson and the case that stunned a nation.

St. Martin's True Crime Library gives you the stories *behind* the headlines. Our authors take you right to the scene of the crime and into the minds of the most notorious murderers to show you what really makes them tick. St. Martin's True Crime Library paperbacks are better than the most terrifying thriller, because it's all true! The next time you want a crackling good read, make sure it's got the St. Martin's True Crime Library logo on the spine—you'll be up all night!

Charles E. Spicer, Jr.
Senior Editor, St. Martin's True Crime Library

"I WANT A GIRL!"

Gerald spat the words at Charlene that cool spring morning. Charlene, adjusting her eyes to the sun rays seeping through the blinds in their bedroom, knew exactly what he meant. If his voice did not tell her, the cold hunger in his eyes did.

It had been exactly ten months since Brenda Judd and Sandra Colley had been abducted, sexually assaulted, and beaten to death. Charlene had nearly disassociated herself from it.

Now Gerry wanted to put her through this all over again. Not to mention some new, helpless victims.

"Get up!" demanded Gerald. Charlene dragged herself out of bed. There was simply no escaping Gerry's warped sexual urges.

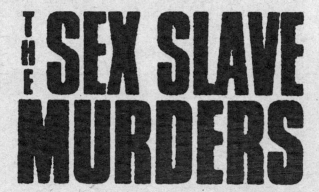

THE SEX SLAVE MURDERS

R. BARRI FLOWERS

St. Martin's Paperbacks

Published by arrangement with J. Flores Publications.

THE SEX SLAVE MURDERS

Copyright © 1995 by Ronald Barri Flowers.

Library of Congress Catalog Card Number: 94-72114

ISBN: 0-312-95989-3

Printed in the United States of America

J. Flores trade paperback edition published in 1995
St. Martin's Paperbacks edition/October 1996

St. Martin's Paperbacks are published by St. Martin's Press, 175 Fifth Avenue, New York, NY 10010.

10 9 8 7 6 5

In memory of Mary, Craig, Virginia, Rhonda, Kippi, Brenda, Sandra, Karen, Stacy, Linda, an unborn child, and others whose lives were cut short, prematurely and tragically. Gone but not forgotten . . .

FOREWORD

When you think of serial killers, probably the first thought to come to mind is "Jack the Ripper," the quintessential serial killer of London's East End in the late 1800s. Also known as the Butcher of Whitechapel, this undiscovered psychopath was credited with the mutilation murders of five prostitutes. As a Ripperologist and criminologist, I have developed over the years a keen interest in trying to analyze and theorize these types of senseless and brutal cold-blooded criminals.

The more recent and closer to home examples include Ted Bundy, John Gacy, Wayne Williams, and Jeffrey Dahmer. In each case the common elements are that the killers are male and the crimes were sexually motivated.

Then there is the story of Gerald and Charlene

Gallego, a husband-wife serial killing team that appears to fit in a class all by themselves. For over a twenty-six-month period between 1978 and 1980, the pair went on a reign of terror covering three states, including kidnapping, sexual assault, torture, and murder. It was the couple's "sex slave" fantasies that led to the brutal deaths of nine women, one man, and one unborn child. Even more frightening is the realization that had it not been for a fortuitous stroke of luck, the two might still be fulfilling their macabre fantasies, while keeping law enforcement at a safe and unsuspecting distance.

I first became interested in this bizarre true crime in early November 1980, when it was reported over the local news that a young couple, Craig Miller and Mary Beth Sowers, was missing after attending a fraternity function. Having only recently moved to Citrus Heights—a suburb of Sacramento where two other Gallego victims were abducted—fresh from college graduation and newly married to my college sweetheart, I found myself piqued by the unfolding story. Before the month was out, both Miller and Sowers were found shot to death. Arrested for their kidnapping and murders were another couple, Gerald and Charlene Gallego.

Both my wife and I felt an instant connection with the slain couple and were appalled that this had happened in a place where we had come to escape the problems of the big city. It was not lost on us that had we been in the wrong place at the wrong time, we might well have suffered the tragic misfortune of Sowers and Miller.

Later we were to learn that the couple was in fact the tenth, eleventh, and final victims of the Gallegos.

More than a decade later, the victims long laid to rest and the killers behind bars, the personal and professional sides of me felt compelled to write the truth-is-stranger-than-fiction story of the Gallegos' reign of terror. As a research criminologist, I have written numerous books and articles that examine criminality, victimization, present statistics, and hypotheses.

This particular project—my first true crime book as it relates to a specific case of criminal behavior—proved to be much more challenging, intense, and at times emotional. Trying to uncover the truth in a crime that involved so many victims, investigators, states, and twists and turns, took some doing.

However, I am confident that what you are about to read on the following pages is as accurate an account of the events that took place as is possible. My research includes court transcripts, medical examiner's reports, police information, prison records, media coverage, cross-checking of dates, times, and places, and hours and hours of leg and phone work.

Out of respect for privacy, the names have been changed of some living characters whose role in the scheme of things is secondary or minimal to the true story.

This book is dedicated to Mary Elizabeth Sowers and Craig Miller and all the other victims of Gerald and Charlene Gallego.

Special thanks goes to my other half, H. Loraine, who in many ways is just as responsible for the conception of this project in November 1980 as bringing it to fruition years later.

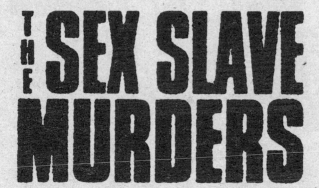

PROLOGUE

Gerald Albert Gallego was nineteen when his son Gerald Armond Gallego was born on July 17, 1946. The elder Gallego was serving time in California's San Quentin prison for auto theft and writing bad checks. He was paroled in February 1949, after serving three years and three months.

By April 1950, Gallego was back behind bars at San Quentin, this time for second-degree robbery. Paroled in October of 1953, Gallego's parole was revoked a few months later, but he managed to evade the law long enough to flee California.

He ended up in Mississippi. On May 27, 1954, Gallego was arrested in Ocean Springs, Mississippi on a charge of drunkenness. As the town's single peace officer, Night Marshall Ernest Beaugez was opening a cell in the Pascagoula, Mississippi jail when Gallego overpowered, disarmed, and kidnapped him.

Beaugez was found murdered by his own gun a few days later. Gallego was apprehended following an armed robbery in another Mississippi town. He was tried, convicted, and sentenced to death for the Beaugez murder. Gallego's execution date was set for March 3, 1955.

On September 10, 1954, Gallego and another death row inmate, Minor Sorber, escaped from the Hinds County jail where they were awaiting their dates with the executioner. In the process, Gallego threw blinding acid disinfectant into the eyes of the jailer, Jack Landrum, and proceeded to severely beat him into unconsciousness. He died four days later.

Gallego and Sorber were recaptured the same day Landrum died. On March 3, 1955, Gerald Albert Gallego, now a convicted murderer of two lawmen, became the first person executed in Mississippi's Parchman Penitentiary's new gas chamber (it replaced the electric chair).

Gallego apparently underwent a religious conversion before he died and became a born-again Christian. As he took his last walk to the gas chamber, Gallego handed Sheriff Leo Byrd of Pascagoula, Mississippi a letter.

It read in part:

> *"Sheriff, if at any time you should have young men in your jail, please tell them that I was once like them, and should they continue, there is no reward but hardships and grief for their parents.*
>
> *Show them the way to God, for God forgives all our sins, and tell them it's nothing to be ashamed of and to humble yourself before God. May my words help those who are on the wrong path . . .*
>
>

Yours in Christ, Gerald A. Gallego"

The father and son were never to meet among the living . . .

ONE

It began as a fairly quiet early Sunday morning of November 2, 1980 in California's capital city. By the end of the day, two lives would be lost forever and many others changed indelibly.

A gateway between the bustle of the San Francisco Bay area, the idyllic beauty of the Sierra Nevada and the gambling meccas of Lake Tahoe and Reno, Sacramento offered perhaps the best of all worlds. It retained much of its cultural and rural past, while steadily becoming an urban and suburban center with an eye on the future.

Arden Fair was an indication of Sacramento catering to its middle class and modernization, with nice homes, popular stores, and new businesses popping up. On this tepid Saturday night, the Arden Fair shopping center was the place to be, particularly if you happened to be the correct fraternity or sorority member at California State University, Sacramento. The Carousel restaurant, located on the east end of the shopping center, had been transformed for the night/morning into a Founder's Day dinner-dance celebration, courtesy of Sigma Phi Epsilon.

Among those attending were CSUS seniors Craig Miller, twenty-two, and Mary Elizabeth Sowers, twenty-one. The all-American couple by nearly every account, they were engaged to be married on New Year's Eve 1981. For Sowers and Miller, hope seemed eternal.

Mary Beth Sowers fit all the adjectives of admiration or envy: beautiful, bright, outgoing, ambitious, warm, sensitive, in love with the world around her and the man she planned to marry. "She was somebody that had a lot of bubble and a lot of sparkle in the way she talked," said a close friend and fellow member of Alpha Chi Omega, the sorority Sowers joined in 1979. "You got more than just words when she talked. You got her feelings and her thoughts."

Mary Beth graduated from Sequoia High School in Redwood City in 1978. Her father was a nuclear physicist at ITEL Corporation in Palo Alto. Following graduation, she moved to Redding, California to attend junior college. There she won the title of runner-up in the Miss Shasta County contest.

Sowers began her junior year at CSUS, majoring in Finance. Despite a full course load, she worked during the week at Arco Financial Services and on weekends at J. C. Penney to support herself. Later, she worked as a ski instructor on weekends at Boreal Ridge, a ski area east of Sacramento. Her talents also included being an expert seamstress, one weekend tailoring three suits.

Mary Beth began dating Craig Miller in late fall of 1979. Theirs was described by friends as a relationship of equals. Noted one friend: "It's so hard to find two people in the same relationship that are that much alike. So dynamic, outgoing, and personable."

Craig Miller graduated from La Sierra High School in 1976. Two years later he graduated from American River College before attending CSUS, where he was on the dean's list. Like Sowers, he seemed tireless, with the sky the limit. Aside from being an accounting executive at Miller Advertising, Miller was vice president of the campus chapter of Sigma Phi Epsilon and the 1979 Man of the Year.

By Mary Elizabeth Sowers's twenty-first birthday on October 21, 1980, she and Craig Miller had been dating for nearly a year. With a spring graduation coming up, marriage plans did not seem premature. New Year's Eve 1981 seemed the perfect wedding day for the couple because New Year's Eve was Mary Beth's favorite day.

On the night of the Sigma Phi Epsilon fraternity function, Craig and Mary Beth arrived late, favoring some quiet time together over the dinner that started three hours prior to their arrival.

That did not mean they weren't looking to make the most of their outing, in the spirit of true fraternity and sorority members. From every indication, Miller and Sowers were happy and content on this night. According to dance attendee, Sheryl Arkin, neither shied from attention. "She had barely gotten in the door," said Arkin of Sowers, "and five of the Alpha Chi pledges were around her in a circle. She was just talking away."

Nevertheless, Craig and Mary Beth's stay was relatively short. They left the Carousel restaurant just after midnight. Shortly thereafter, a fraternity brother happened by chance to notice Miller and Sowers in the back of an Oldsmobile Cutlass rather than Sowers's red Honda.

After an exchange of words between the fraternity brother and the front seat occupants of the car—a woman was in the driver's seat with a man beside her—the Oldsmobile sped off, with Miller and Sowers still in the back seat.

This was the last time Craig and Mary Beth were seen alive.

*   *   *

That afternoon, Craig Miller's body was discovered alongside a gravel road twenty miles from Placerville, near Bass Lake in El Dorado County, California. He had been shot three times at point-blank range. An autopsy performed the following day revealed that Miller had been shot once above the right ear, once in the back of the neck, and once at the right cheekbone—apparently at the site.

Mary Elizabeth Sowers was still missing.

As with many non-domestic crimes of violence, solving such crimes often takes a combination of police investigative work and a bit of luck. In this instance, the luck came with a license plate number taken down by a concerned friend who thought it unusual that Craig Miller and his fiancee, Mary Elizabeth Sowers, would take off with strangers in the wee hours of the morning of November 2, 1980 from the Arden Fair shopping center parking lot, leaving Sowers's red Honda behind.

When the couple failed to return to the Honda by that afternoon, the friend and fellow member of Miller's fraternity reported them missing. Tracing the license number of the car Miller and Sowers disappeared in, the police discovered that the car—a silver 1977 Oldsmobile Cutlass—was registered to Charlene A. Williams or Charles Williams, her father. This was the second big break.

In the meantime, Miller's mother worried that her usually dependable son and future daughter-in-law were missing. A friend of Sowers had phoned Miller's mother early Sunday morning looking for Miller. "I don't want you to worry," the friend had said, "but something really strange is going on. Nobody has seen Mary Beth or Craig since last night."

When Miller failed to show up for his 10:00 A.M. shift at a paint store in Carmichael, his mother telephoned police.

After learning from the Department of Motor Vehicles that the Oldsmobile Cutlass belonged to Charlene A. Williams or Charles Williams, Detective Lee Taylor and Detective Larry Burchett drove to the home of Charles and Mercedes Williams on Berrendo Drive in Arden Park.

The parents told the detectives that the Cutlass was their daughter Charlene's, and that she had left home about 6:30 P.M. Saturday to go to a movie theater with her boyfriend, Stephen Robert Feil. During the conversation, Charlene drove up in her silver Cutlass. This was the third big break, although it did not seem like it at the time.

Charlene, twenty-four, was blonde, pretty, petite, and seven months pregnant. She denied any knowledge of the disappearance of Sowers or Miller. She allowed the detectives to search the

Cutlass. They found no indication of foul play or otherwise incriminating evidence that a crime had been committed.

Charlene complained of being sick because of her pregnancy and suffering from a hangover. She gave few details about her boyfriend, Stephen Feil.

The detectives, unaware that Miller's body was soon to be discovered and having no other reason to detain the ill Charlene further, promised to return later that day to photograph her. She, in turn, hoped to have recovered somewhat and be more cooperative.

It was not until the following day that Charles and Mercedes Williams admitted to the detectives that their daughter was married to Stephen Feil and that this was actually an alias used by Gerald Gallego, thirty-four, who was wanted on incest and other sex charges.

Suddenly some frightening pieces of a bizarre puzzle began to fall into place. Not only had the Gallegos become the chief suspects in the murder of Craig Miller and disappearance of Mary Beth Sowers, but it seemed that neighboring Yolo County authorities were also investigating the connection of a Stephen Feil to the kidnapping-murder of Virginia Mochel, a local bartender.

Unfortunately, by now the Gallegos, sensing trouble, had fled to parts unknown.

On November 5, 1980, El Dorado County filed charges of kidnapping and murder against Gerald and Charlene Gallego. The following day, a federal fugitive warrant of unlawful flight to avoid prosecution was issued against the Gallegos to allow the FBI to join in a nationwide search for the fugitive couple.

That search came to an end twelve days later. On Monday, November 17, 1980, Gerald and Charlene Gallego were captured by FBI agents in Omaha, Nebraska, while they were attempting to pick up money that had been wired to them by Charlene's parents at a Western Union office in downtown Omaha.

The arrest came without incidence and brought to an end what was later discovered to be a twenty-six-month reign of sex-motivated brutality and murder.

Yet this was only the beginning of a bizarre tale of sexual fantasies, domination, and terror that was to unravel and take three and a half more years to complete.

TWO

The two seemed as unlikely for each other as they did a couple capable of being, quite possibly, this country's first husband-and-wife serial killers.

Physically speaking, Gerald and Charlene Gallego were definitely mismatched. He was a shade over five-seven, with rugged features, a stump of a neck, and deep dark eyes. His brown hair was parted to one side, slicked down the other. An ape-like build seemed to dwarf his wife, who stood at five feet and barely tipped the scales at one hundred pounds.

Charlene looked like a Barbie doll. Cute, blonde-haired, blue-eyed, diminutive, sweet, innocent . . . She probably could have had any man she wanted—and took advantage of that at least twice in marriages prior to Gerald. Indeed, this was the one practice the two had in common as Gerald had gone down the aisle a minimum of five times prior to ever laying eyes on Charlene.

Their earlier backgrounds present two vastly different lives before they defied the odds and became a pair. Gerald Armond Gallego was born on July 17, 1946 in Sacramento, the offspring of Gerald Albert and Lorraine Gallego.

If there was ever a case of being born to kill, figuratively speaking, Gerald number two's name was on the birth certificate. He came from a long line of violent career criminals on both sides of the family.

Probably no one was more violent than his own father, Gerald Albert, whom he never had the pleasure of meeting. The elder Gerald, a convicted multiple murderer, was executed in Mississippi's gas chamber in March 1955. His mother remarried twice following Gallego's death. Court records indicate that Gerald rarely got along with his stepfathers. Gerald number two was nine at the time of his father's death and well on his way to following in his father's footsteps.

Gerald Armond Gallego's criminal record began at age six, and included everything from running away to various sex offenses to burglary. At age twelve, he was placed on probation by the juvenile authorities for burglary and later charged with committing lewd and lascivious acts with a six-year-old girl. This landed him in a California Youth Authority (CYA) facility, Fred C. Nelles School for Boys, in October 1959. Paroled in July 1961, he was arrested again less than a year later, along with his half-brother, David Hunt, for armed robbery and sentenced to the Preston School of Industry in Ione, California. Gerald escaped shortly thereafter, turned himself in, and was eventually paroled in 1963.

School proved to be equally frustrating for Gerald Gallego. He was suspended from Sacramento High School in December 1963 after receiving five Fs in classes and behavior. According to his probation officer at the time, he was considered a habitual truant whose suspension was for truancy, tardiness, profanity, and violating closed-campus rules. The probation officer's report concluded: "His social traits were all listed as failures. He currently typifies a hard-shelled young man who evidenced little motivation for improvement, remorsefulness, or insight."

Gerald Gallego's troubles with the law continued into adulthood. Often bragging to friends about getting away with crimes ranging from stealing cars to holding up drugstores, Gerald and his half-brother, David, were finally arrested on October 25, 1969, during an armed robbery of a motel in Vacaville, California. The half-brothers and another inmate escaped from the Solano County jail shortly thereafter and were recaptured four days later in San Francisco.

Gallego was sentenced to serve five years to life in state prison. He started his term at the Deuel Vocational Institution at Tracy before being transferred to the California Medical Facility in Vacaville for psychiatric treatment for depression.

By the time Gerald Gallego met Charlene Williams, he had been arrested no less than twenty-three times.

By comparison to Gerald's early years, Charlene led a charmed life. Charlene Adell Williams was born on October 19, 1956 in Stockton, California, a quiet, rural town about fifty miles from Sacramento. An only child, she was the apple of her parents', Charles and Mercedes Williams, and grandparents' eyes. Whatever their little girl with the golden pigtails wanted was usually there for the asking.

This was made possible by Charles Williams's incredible success, going from a supermarket butcher to a top executive for another supermarket chain with outlets across the country. Mercedes supplemented his income by selling cosmetics. The family ultimately moved from Stockton to the upper-middle-class Arden Park area of Sacramento.

By most accounts, Charlene grew up shy and

aloof, calling little attention to herself. Unlike her future husband, Charlene had never been arrested or accused of any crime, much less served any time prior to that fateful day of November 17, 1980.

Indeed, her early years showed much promise. An unusually high IQ led her to being placed in a sixth-grade class for gifted students. Two years earlier she had learned to play the violin with such passion that daddy purchased her a violin of her own, and there was talk of her someday attending the Juilliard School of Music. She seemed to be a natural leader among students and eagerly participated in various extracurricular activities.

It was not until Charlene started attending Rio Americano High School that changes began to occur in her personality, habits, and bright potential. A predilection for sex, drugs, alcohol, and rebellion seemed to all but ruin the edge she had once enjoyed over other students. Her grades began to tumble to the point where graduation, once a foregone conclusion, became a struggle in which she barely succeeded.

The one thing Charlene still had going for her was a father who would do anything to please his favorite girl. After she graduated, he bought her a shiny new Oldsmobile (which would later come back to haunt her), put her into her own apartment, and helped improve her wardrobe when she saw fit to buy new clothes, which was often. He even went so far as to invest $15,000 in "The Dingaling Shop," Charlene's on-a-whim business venture in which she rented a 10 × 12 foot space in a Folsom shopping strip. There she sold potted plants, macrame, and knickknacks.

Unfortunately for Charlene's eager-to-please daddy, her attention and desires quickly moved elsewhere.

The one thing Gerald Gallego did seem to have going for him was his charm and appeal as a ladies' man. Before Charlene entered his life, and after, he seemed to have little trouble attracting women, in spite of a violent streak that he usually took out on those whom he lulled into a very false sense of security.

"He was the type of guy any girl would want," claimed one ex-girlfriend. Other women described him as "Mr. Macho." Women were known to phone him regularly during his bartending days in Sacramento and he would rate them "number one girl," "number two girl" . . .

A former wife admitted: "He's not good looking, but he sure can make a woman feel like a woman . . . He has that type of magnetism."

Another ex-wife recalled a far more dark side to Gallego, labeling him: "A perverted psychosexual maniac." She went on to say it was like "being in bed with a rabid Tasmanian Devil," whose only

interests in sex were "sodomy, fellatio, and cunni-
lingus—in that order."

Of Gallego's five wives that preceded Charlene,
each and every one became a battered wife, often
abused emotionally and financially as well. Gerald's first marriage took place in 1963. He was sixteen, she was twenty-one. In April of 1964, his first
child, Krista, was born.

The marriage was short-lived after the wife was
subjected to beatings with Gerald's fists and a hammer. Both parents fought tooth and nail for custody
of their daughter. Ultimately Gerald gained custody and sent Krista to live with his mother. (Later
it turned out that his motives were anything but
fatherly, and had indirectly played a role in his sex
slave fantasies that turned into kidnapping, rape,
and murder.)

Marriage number two occurred on July 12, 1966,
to a twenty-four-year-old West Sacramento wait-
ress. Only twenty-six days of marriage passed before the bride saw Gerald's true colors and left him.
"He chased me all over the house that day with a
knife," she recalled. "I locked myself in the bathroom and he finally calmed down. I was going to
leave then and he wouldn't let me out of the
house."

Gallego's third wife, a laundry worker, found it
almost too painful to talk about their tumultuous
marriage. "I've blocked all that out for years," she

19

stammered. "It's such a horrible memory." They had wed on October 14, 1967. "He kept beating me. I couldn't take it. He became very cruel."

The marriage lasted only one month.

Marriage number four for Gerald took place in Reno in March 1969. Harriette, nineteen, was pregnant when the marriage ended less than a month later. Her father, speaking on behalf of his daughter, said of Gallego:

"He was a Jekyll and Hyde. He was such a nice boy when he was coming to the house. Then they got married. Nineteen days later, I wanted to kill him."

As far as it is known, Harriette's daughter still does not know who her real father is.

Gallego went down the aisle a fifth time in Butte County on October 5, 1974. His wife, nineteen, was a laundress. The minister who performed the ceremony remembered that a young girl, Krista, had served as ring bearer. She had been introduced as Gerald's sister. In fact, she was his now ten-year-old daughter by his first marriage.

Gerald was on parole at this time and had managed to convince his parole agent that he was a reformed man. In recommending that Gerald be released from parole, the agent wrote in a report dated December 5, 1975: ". . . It is the feeling of this agent that he [Gallego] could be discharged from further parole supervision without a significant risk to the community."

On December 12, 1975, Gerald Gallego became a free man from the system of justice. This grave error in judgement was to come back to haunt the parole agent and many others.

Gerald separated from wife number five in August of 1977. When he made Charlene his sixth wife, his divorce from the fifth was still two months away from being finalized.

Charlene Williams did not fare much better when it came to marriage. She celebrated her eighteenth birthday on October 19, 1974, by marrying a nineteen-year-old soldier named Rick. One day later, Rick reported for army duty in Germany. The marriage was annulled shortly thereafter at the petition of Rick's parents.

According to Rick, he and Charlene met while he was on a weekend home leave in Sacramento. He had become quickly attracted to Charlene, he said, because she was "very quiet, soft spoken, very graceful . . . her manners were perfect." Then he noticed a big change in her just before their "spur of the moment" marriage. "She had a hairdresser cut and style her hair, she began using makeup, and she started dressing with flair."

Upon arriving in Germany, Rick claimed to have written Charlene "almost daily," but received no response. The annulment was granted on May 5, 1975.

In the meantime, Charlene had decided to give college a try by enrolling at California State University in the fall of 1974. Her major was psychology. This lark lasted one semester before she dropped out.

Marriage number two came for Charlene on August 29, 1976, in a ceremony attended by over one hundred guests at a United Methodist Church in Sacramento. The groom, Elliot, was a twenty-four-year-old ex-soldier whom Charlene had met while a high school senior and had dated off and on.

During their brief but stormy marriage, both Charlene and Elliot encountered health problems. Charlene suffered from bronchial asthma, said Elliot, which he believed she used as "a crutch to lean on . . . if something didn't go right." He described himself as an epileptic, subject to violent seizures.

He also admitted to drug use, sometimes heavy, and accused Charlene of the same, along with alcohol abuse. He recalled them attending a party and smoking marijuana, which they later learned had been sprinkled with PCP, an animal tranquilizer that severely distorts perception and causes violent behavior. He also claimed Charlene had taken LSD, a psychedelic drug particularly popular in the seventies.

According to Elliot, Charlene once tried to commit suicide during their marriage by ingesting Pine-Sol disinfectant. "She opened the doggone thing up and stuck it in her mouth," he said. "That's when I knocked it right out of her mouth, otherwise she would have drank it."

Elliot attributed at least part of their problems to Charlene's attentive parents. "They were more or less interfering with our marriage," he said. "They were trying to tell me what I could do, what I couldn't do. They kept pushing and pushing, causing problems."

The marriage officially ended on May 25, 1977.

In the fall of 1977, Charlene Williams met Gerald Gallego. Neither could have imagined what a lethal combination they were about to make.

THREE

The news that the Gallegos had been captured by
FBI agents in Nebraska was headline material
the following day for much of the western United
States, comforted with the knowledge that this couple, suspected of ruining the dreams of another
couple, was now behind bars.

What few realized—at least those alive to talk
about it—was that the confirmed death of Craig
Miller and suspected death of Mary Beth Sowers
was but the tip of the iceberg. Gerald and Charlene
Gallego had deep, sordid secrets that would shock
the nation and tie together a string of unresolved
disappearances and murder investigations covering three states.

Two hours after their arrest, Gerald Gallego and
his seven months pregnant wife, Charlene, ap-

peared before U.S. Magistrate Richard Peck in
Omaha. Assistant U.S. Attorney Thomas Thalken
argued that bail should be set at $500,000 for each
defendant, noting the particularly brutal nature of
the one crime known to have been committed for
sure.

Peck, not allowing theatrics or as-yet-unknown
future physical evidence to cloud his judgement,
set bail at $100,000 for each defendant and said that
attorneys would be furnished if they could not afford their own.

One of the U.S. marshalls who had escorted Gerald Gallego into court spoke up that Mr. Gallego
had refused to cooperate in being fingerprinted
and processed.

Gerald was quick to defend his actions. "Your
Honor," he grumbled, "I didn't cooperate because
I was viciously pulled off the street by FBI agents."
He snarled at the marshall. "They handcuffed me
so tight my circulation was cut off." He then com-
plained that they "threw me into a jail cell."

If Peck was at all moved by Gallego's complaints,
he was not about to show it.

Gerald claimed to be unaware of the California
warrants until they were arrested. "Your Honor, I
... we ... want to return to California to square
things away."

Peck seemed more than happy to oblige. But
there were still the formalities. He set a hearing for

the following day to decide if there was sufficient evidence for the Gallegos to be detained or extradited to California to face the charges filed by El Dorado County.

Mary Beth Sowers had been missing for nearly three weeks now. Despite fearing the worst, her family clung to the hope that she might still be alive.

To that end, they issued a plea for information to anyone who might be able to offer even a clue as to her whereabouts or condition:

It is impossible to express the feelings of her [Mary Beth's] family under such conditions. We are emotionally at the bottom of human resources. Our children have been devastated by this bizarre event. It is a fact that we survive now on our faith in God and belief in Mary Beth's strength of survival and the enormous concern and prayers of our and Mary Beth's friends.

The amount of energy that is being put forth to sustain us and Mary Beth through these friends is surely beyond any measurable quantity. Such an experience is so draining on all of us that it is reaching the stage of emotional destruction.

We desperately need help from anyone who knows anything about this case and we speak directly to Gerald and Charlene Gallego . . . their at-

torney, and Mrs. Gallego's parents. There is no way they can begin to relate to the pain that we are suffering from not knowing, and how much more difficult it becomes each passing minute.

Waiting under such conditions has to be one of the most excruciating of all tortures.

We need public support to bring pressure to bear in any way that would help resolve Mary Beth's situation.

We make our plea for help through God for all our family, friends, and the many people who have prayed deeply for Mary Beth's safe return.

The statement was signed by Mary Beth's family.

The Gallegos, being held at the Douglas County Correctional Center in Omaha, seemed in no hurry to talk about Mary Beth Sowers's fate nor the murder of Craig Miller. On the advice of an attorney retained by Charles and Mercedes Williams, Gerald and Charlene were more silent than either suspect could probably stand, given the overlapping thoughts that surely were going through their minds.

At their hearing, the Gallegos waived extradition proceedings and agreed to return to California voluntarily. They were being charged with the kidnapping and murder of twenty-two-year-old Craig

Miller, and the kidnapping of twenty-one-year-old Mary Elizabeth Sowers.

If there was a ray of light for the suspects, it occurred earlier in the day when federal charges of unlawful flight to avoid prosecution for murder were dismissed.

Officers from El Dorado County and Sacramento were dispatched to Nebraska to escort the newly infamous married couple back to California.

On Saturday, November 22, 1980, the worst-case scenario on the fate of Mary Beth Sowers was realized. Just before three P.M., two young men target shooting in a field in Placer County discovered the badly decomposed body of a young woman lying in a shallow trench. She was wearing a purplish-blue silk evening gown that matched the description of the one the missing coed was wearing the night of the Sigma Phi Epsilon Founder's Day dinner-dance. The two young men, who both lived in the area, immediately drove to the home of Placer County Sheriff Donald Nunes and reported their grisly discovery.

During an autopsy the following day, the victim was positively identified as Mary Elizabeth Sowers by Dr. James Nordstrom of Auburn, an expert in forensic dentistry, after studying her dental charts. The autopsy further revealed that Mary Beth, whose hands were bound behind her back, had been shot three times in the head, just as her fiance, Craig Miller, had.

The new charge of the murder of Mary Beth Sowers had been added to those Gerald and Charlene Gallego already faced.

FOUR

Whatever the odds may have been for Gerald Armond Gallego and Charlene Adell Williams ever meeting, they somehow managed to beat them. It was in mid-September 1977 that they first laid eyes on one another.

Charlene, just a month or so shy of her twenty-first birthday, celebrated prematurely at the Black Stallion Card Room, a less than savory but licensed poker club in Sacramento. Exactly what she had in mind in going to the club in the first place is still in question. Some had her there to buy cocaine from a drug dealer friend. Others said she was there simply to drink, dance, and have fun. Yet another theory put her there to meet a blind date by the name of Gerald Gallego.

The last version comes closest to Charlene's own

account. According to her, she met Gerald at the club through one of his relatives.

"I thought he was a very nice, clean-cut fellow," Charlene would say several years later.

Whatever she saw in him, it pleased her, as it had the many women who came before Charlene in Gerald's life. This man was charming, attentive, slick, muscular, and intriguing to a twenty-year-old going on thirty.

Gerald obviously had his own attraction to the cute blue-eyed blonde with the girl-next-door looks. She was also small, thin, and cuddly, just the way he liked his women. Yet it is doubtful that Gerald—a man married five times, who had probably romanced ten times as many other girls and women—saw anything more in Charlene at the beginning than a temporary but appealing distraction.

When he politely asked for her phone number, she was flattered and quick to oblige. The next day, she received a dozen long-stemmed red roses with a note that read: "To a very sweet girl. Gerry."

From that point on, Charlene Williams was sold on this man, and he intended to take full advantage of it. Within weeks, they were living together in a duplex Charlene was renting on Mission Avenue. And the troubles began.

Gerald was a con artist all the way. He knew what it took to mesmerize women into seeing things his way. But once he had captured the golden goose, there was no damned reason he could think of for maintaining his facade of being "considerate, polite, and fun to be with." As with the other women in his life, he soon became domineering and demanding of his new girlfriend.

"I was supposed to do what I was told," Charlene would later testify.

Her boyfriend had suddenly become critical of her personality and mannerisms. He was no longer satisfied with what she thought was a fashionable hairstyle. He ordered her to wear her hair with bangs and in pigtails. And her clothes, many of which daddy had purchased for her in her constant desire to keep up with the Joneses, were now unappealing to Gerry. He had her wearing jeans and T-shirts.

Then there was the money thing. Charlene was working at a supermarket, only to sign her earnings over to her live-in lover. His own contribution to their financial livelihood consisted of some occasional money made playing cards. But far more tended to be lost from his shuffling of the deck.

As far as Charlene was concerned, their problems really arose in the bedroom. She liked sex as much as any woman—probably more—and she did what she could to please her man sexually. It was never enough, though. If there was a problem—which often was the case—it was her fault.

Gerry had problems getting an erection. He blamed her. They would try every position known to man—and some known only to Gerry—and he would still be left limp. And angry. He would tell her she wasn't doing something right or doing something wrong. If he wanted a particular type of sex and she said it hurt, he would tell her: "That's too damned bad!"

As if their sex life at home was not frustrating enough, Charlene also had to contend with Gerry's roving eye and constant comparisons between her and other women. He had his rating system: "Number one girl, number two girl . . ." She was never good enough to make the top of the list, but he seemed to take delight in putting her at the bottom. If he was in a generous mood, she might make it as his "number two girl."

Charlene had her doubts as to whether she would ever measure up to his silly ratings or "the girl with heart," as he would say. But she was committed to continue to try to please this man she had so quickly fallen in love with and felt she would do anything for.

Unlike the two weak "mamma's boys" Charlene had married, there was a certain strength and confidence about Gerry. She liked that and wanted to hold on to it, even if the price was something she was far from comfortable with.

In time, she believed he would ask her to marry

him. The third time had to be the charm.

In December of 1977, Charlene purchased a .25 caliber FIE automatic pistol at a sporting goods store in Del Paso Heights. It was an omen of things to come.

Gerald moved out of the duplex in the spring of 1978. Unfortunately for Charlene, he returned a few weeks later. It was sometime during his absence, and perhaps because of it, that Gerald began to give serious thought to his sexual fantasies and now wanted to share them with Charlene.

"I have this fantasy," he told her, "about having girls that would be there whenever I wanted them and do whatever I wanted them to. They have to be young, too," he added, "ripe for the picking."

"That'll only happen in your dreams, Gerry," Charlene told him. She had no reason to believe that his erotic fantasies were anything more than wishful thinking and, therefore, harmless. She saw them as "competition for real love" in which she might well be facing a losing battle.

In April 1978, Charlene and Gerald accompanied her parents to the annual grocer's banquet in Sacramento. Charles Williams used the opportunity to introduce his daughter's boyfriend to a business associate of a local meat company. Always thinking of Charlene's well-being—which in this case meant helping Gerald find work—Charles Williams was not above using any connections he had to please her.

Within a few weeks, the connection came through. Gerald was offered a job as a route driver for the meat company at a salary of $11 an hour, which he accepted. In the meantime, he had rented his own apartment on Watt Avenue and was living with his daughter, Krista, now fourteen. Two days before Gerald began his new job, a fourteen-year-old friend of Krista's from Chico named Angie came to visit for a couple of weeks. Angie would later tell authorities that she had been sexually molested by Gerald twice during her visit.

His sexual fantasies had begun to come to fruition.

And so had Charlene's. At twenty-one, she was like many others her age still exploring their sexuality. She had shown an interest in women since before she had met Gerald. An ex-husband noted her fantasies of "being raped by another woman" and "going to bed with a whore."

By the summer of 1978, Charlene put her fantasies to the test for perhaps the first time. Surprising Charlene, Gerald decided to pay her a visit after work one day and caught her in bed with a woman. Actually, the woman was not quite eighteen yet. Things just happened, rationalized Charlene, then sort of got out of hand.

Gerald went crazy. He hated gays. He couldn't

understand how two people of the same sex could have sex or even want to. During his first trial, he actually used this episode in his defense as a desperate and ridiculous attempt to call into question, or morality, Charlene's credibility as the prosecution's star witness against him.

The greater wound, though, was to his male ego. Gerald considered himself more than enough man for any woman. His impotence was not likely to improve any time soon.

Gerald physically abused Charlene and her lover while shouting expletives, kicked the lover out, and gave Charlene a second dose of his overpowering rage.

On July 17, 1978, Gerald celebrated his thirty-second birthday by sodomizing his daughter. She later testified that her father had sexually molested her since she was six, also noting that Charlene had been in the house during some of the molestations.

It was almost time for Gallego to move his sexual fantasies to another level.

Charlene got pregnant in July of 1978, much to Gerald's chagrin. It threatened to interfere with his plans.

"Why the hell didn't you do something so you wouldn't get pregnant?" he barked at her.

"It's not my fault, Gerry," she cried.

"It sure as hell isn't mine," he retorted unsympathetically.

He neither wanted nor needed any more kids in his life. He could hardly keep up with the ones he had, some he probably didn't even know about.

This unborn bastard had to go.

By the end of the month, Gerald's trucking job was in jeopardy. "He couldn't hack it," said his employer. "He couldn't do the job . . . he was really inadequate."

On August 2, 1978, under pressure, Gerald quit his job. A couple of weeks later, Krista moved back in with Gerald's mother in Chico.

FIVE

The sex slave fantasy took a brutal and deadly turn on September 11, 1978. That was the day Gerald Gallego decided it was time to bring his fantasies to life—even if it meant it would cost others their lives in the process.

He had been regularly molesting his daughter during those visits to Chico over the summer, but it was not enough to fulfill his growing desires. Not by a long shot.

He woke up the one that was to be his partner in crime and the bait for his sex slaves.

Charlene, now two months pregnant, had been experiencing morning sickness. She seemed particularly sick on this day. That was *her* problem as far as Gerry was concerned. She had to get up *now*, for he had plans that she was not going to screw up.

Charlene dragged herself out of bed and got dressed. Gerry had a funny look on his face at the kitchen table as he loaded the FIE .25 caliber pistol she'd purchased for him last December. Even then, Charlene believed it would be used more as a scare tactic than to actually do bodily harm, much less kill someone.

Gerry was a little—maybe a lot—crazy and violent when things didn't go his way, but he was no killer. She ate while listening as he went over his plans to find some girls to take part in his sex fantasy.

She felt weird in going along with Gerry's strange desire to have his own sex slaves, but Charlene also wanted to please this man she loved. Maybe this whole thing was only a game—a test of love. Maybe this was his way of making her prove she was "the girl with heart" and therefore his "number one girl" . . . ?

Whatever convincing Charlene needed to do within, she did it. And the couple was off to put the plan into action.

They took the 1973 Dodge recreational van that Charlene had purchased with the help of a loan cosigned by her always dependable daddy. Gerry liked the van for its smooth ride and roominess in the back, where he and Charlene sometimes had sex. He also fancied the scenery painted on the sides of the van, which featured a mountainous region with vultures swarming overhead, as if they were zeroing in on their prey.

It was another hot day in the valley as they cruised around town, ending up at the Country Club Plaza shopping center. Gerald drove through the parking lot while giving Charlene instructions once more. She was to search and find some sweet, nubile girls, get them to the van any damned way she could short of dragging them screaming, and he would take over from there.

When Charlene made the mistake of complaining about her morning sickness, he cursed at her in such a way that she did not dare bring it up again. Now was not the time to make him mad.

Gerald went to a store for some adhesive tape while Charlene embarked on her mission. She roamed almost absentmindedly through the mall that seemed overly crowded, looking for prospective volunteers as sex slaves. Or at least to smoke some marijuana—her enticement for them.

Her fears and caution made the task almost impossible at first. Evidently she was taking too long, as Gerry appeared out of nowhere, poked her hard in the side, and asked her out loud: "What the hell are you doing . . . ? Not what you're supposed to be—"

She was surprised he had followed her and spoken so vociferously, as if he wanted to advertise to the whole world just what he had in mind.

"I'm trying, Gerry," she whined.

"Try harder, bitch!" he demanded. "I'll be waiting. Don't let me down—"

And once again she was left alone to do her job.

Admittedly intimidated by her boyfriend and uneasy about stretching this out any longer than necessary, Charlene spotted two girls that seemed tailor-made for Gerald's dark fantasy.

They were young, starry-eyed, pretty—much like her and his favorite daughter, Krista. Yes, they were definitely the ones.

If there was something called fate, there was also something called free will. Charlene had reached that critical moment where the power of life and death was literally in her hands. She could walk away and never look back.

Or she could risk Gerry's definite wrath by disobeying his commands. She probably thought about it for a moment or two . . . before succumbing to Gerald's dominance over her. She approached the two girls who looked to be in their late teens. Maybe even younger.

"Hi," she said cheerfully. "You girls wanna smoke some pot?" Grinning, they were eager to partake.

Like the Pied Piper, she led them to an unsuspecting fate.

*   *   *

Rhonda Scheffler, seventeen, and Kippi Vaught, sixteen, could have been any of millions of adolescents on the brink of adulthood across the country: precocious, rebellious, curious, naive, impressionable—and somewhere, anywhere, else. But they were not on this sizzling afternoon. To their misfortune, they were two teenagers who had been handpicked for a journey in which there would be no return.

Even Gerald Gallego, a man who had been in and out of trouble all his life, had reached a crossroads. It was one thing to rob old ladies. Even beating up on his wives was, in his warped mind, not all that bad as far as the authorities were concerned.

But for what he had in mind, there could be no turning back. He was embarking on an entirely new adventure in which the stakes were ten times as high as any of his other violations of what others called the law. There was no half stepping here. He either was to call it off, tell Charlene it was all a big joke for my "girl with heart," or he had to follow through on his sex slave fantasy.

Then he saw Charlene and the recruits approaching the van. She really had done it—brought him girls who were ripe and ready!

He got excited as he thought about the fantasy that lay in wait for the right time and circumstances.

Suddenly forgotten were his second thoughts.
There could be no backing down now. He was going for it. The hell with everything else. He would
let the damned chips fall where they may.

Rhonda and Kippi stepped into the back of the
van looking for a terrific high. Instead what they
got was a .25 caliber pistol pointed at them by a
man who did not look at all like he was playing
games.

It didn't look that way to Charlene either as Gerald took quick steps to secure his advantage over
the startled and frightened girls. He made the girls
lie face down and then, using the adhesive tape he
had bought, bound their hands and feet.

It was now Charlene's job to watch his sex slaves,
keep them quiet and docile, while he drove them
to an area where he could safely put his fantasies
into practice. Like a good little girl, Charlene
obeyed Gerry's orders, taking a seat on an ice chest
in the back of the van and standing guard over the
hapless, helpless, soon-to-be victims.

Gerald said nothing, not even to Charlene, as he
started the van and negotiated his way out of the
parking lot and onto the street. Soon they pulled
onto Interstate 80, heading east toward the Sierra
Nevada.

Charlene herself was also left speechless. After
all, what the hell could she say? This is all wrong,
Gerry. Let these girls go. They'll never tell a soul

about this and you and I can get on with our
lives . . . ?

Something told her he was not about to call off
his sex slave fantasy—not now that it was well
within his grasp.

But what then? Charlene must have wondered.
How far was he prepared to carry this crazy
scheme? She dared not consider the worst-case scenario—for those girls' sake, and maybe even her
own down the line.

Charlene eyed precariously the two girls who
whimpered and murmured, but otherwise were
fairly well behaved under the circumstances.

They passed by one small town after another before pulling off the interstate at Baxter, a nonde-
script town amidst the Sierra Nevada mountains.
Actually, to those who lived amongst the groves of
pine trees and steep foothills, Baxter was more than
just a highway maintenance station or a dot on the
map. It was a place where the past could be revis-
ited and a family could live in relative tranquility
with the knowledge that Sacramento was but an
hour away whenever one wanted more of the big
city than Baxter would ever offer.

Right now, however, for Rhonda Scheffler and
Kippi Vaught, Baxter was the last place on earth
they wanted to be. It was almost the last place they
ever would be.

Gerald drove the van expertly through and

around the meandering road, across a fragile bridge, and finally found a lush spot off the road that he considered satisfactory to get the job done. The van was brought to a stop and his sex slaves were given his undivided attention.

This was one time when Charlene truly was not the number one or two girl for what he had in mind.

Charlene watched as Gerry unbound the girls' ankles, helped them out of the van, and ordered them to start walking. He pointed in a direction away from the road where the trees made perfect cover and could easily distort sound effects.

"Wait here," he told Charlene, and she did while he trailed his prey. He took with him a sleeping bag, blanket, and the .25 caliber gun.

Charlene might have used the word "boring" to describe her being left all by her lonesome for hours that turned day into dusk. But most likely the time was used to contemplate the fate of the girls. Had Gerry's sex slaves been all he had hoped for? Would this satisfy him or would there be others in the future? What type of sex would he expect from me after his fantasy girls? wondered Charlene. Could I possibly ever compete?

Gerald finally returned—without his sex slaves. His stern look at Charlene told her: "Ask me no questions, I'll tell you no lies."

So she did not inquire. Instead, she listened as

he barked new instructions at her. She was to drive back to Sacramento, make sure she stayed within the speed limit—getting a speeding ticket would not be a smart move for either of them right now—get yourself seen by friends who can vouch for your being there, then get your ass back here—but come in the Oldsmobile.

If Charlene was the least bit confused as to why this back and forth journey, she kept it to herself. She was certain Gerry knew what he was doing. By tomorrow it would be over and they could return to what, for them, was a normal life.

Charlene followed Gerald's orders explicitly. She took the van back to Sacramento, visited an old and onetime dear friend, and said a few wry comments about the condition of the van, before replacing it at the apartment with her Oldsmobile.

The mercury had dropped considerably since she had left the mountains, and Charlene was concerned that Gerry and the girls might be getting cold. So she put the pedal to the metal and ended up in Baxter sooner than she was supposed to be. She decided she feared venting Gerald's wrath for being too early more than his getting frostbite, so she parked near a mostly deserted shopping strip and waited.

If there was ever a time for Charlene to avert further tragedy, which she must surely have realized was a distinct possibility, it came when she noted a passing Highway Patrol car. The patrolman inside noticed her as well.

He could help me, she might have thought. Or better still, help those girls.

This was a path she chose not to pursue. Instead, she tried her best to give the guise that all was well. Hope you have a nice evening, officer, she voiced within while smiling lightly.

The patrolman may have smiled back as he drove off. With him went the last chance two teenagers would ever have to be rescued and returned home—alive.

Charlene waited a moment or two longer before starting the Olds. She followed Gerald's path, parked, and signaled him the way they had prearranged.

He showed up alone. "You don't know how glad I am to see you," he said, his breath lingering in the air from the cold. "I was freezing my ass off out here!"

A tiny smile played on her lips. Then she asked him what had to be asked. "Where are the girls?"

"You'll see," he responded tonelessly, got in beside her, and told her to drive into the woods.

She stopped near a clearing. Gerald got out, disappeared, and returned with the girls. They were ordered into the back seat at gunpoint. Charlene couldn't help but notice that they were disheveled, disoriented, and dirty—but thankfully, still alive. Gerald sat beside them and directed Charlene to hit the road again.

In the meantime, he assured his abducted and violated guests that everything would be fine. No more harm would come to them.

No doubt Charlene wanted to believe Gerry. Enough was enough. Anything more could be downright dangerous for them, their future.

She got back on the highway and headed toward Sacramento. Eventually they reached Sloughhouse, a farming area on the other side of Sacramento County.

Once again, Gerald sought to assure his captives not to worry. "We're just going to make it harder for you to get back," he said in a friendly tone.

He told Charlene to turn this way and that, until she had driven onto a dusty, dark road between fields.

"Here!" his one-word order rang through the car as Charlene stopped on a dime.

Music played on the radio. Any music would do for Gerald. At that point, Charlene would have been satisfied if Gerry had told the girls to get out and don't call the cops, leaving them there with a long walk back to civilization.

However, it was never that cut and dried with Gerry. He made the girls get out and he accompanied them.

"Turn up the radio all the way," he told Charlene, "and don't turn around!"

She swallowed unevenly, and did as she was told. The music was deafening, her gaze straight ahead, even if her mind was elsewhere.

She heard what sounded like pops. Seconds later, Gerald returned to the driver's side window, told her to move over, and sat beside her. He was breathing erratically.

Neither said a word.

Then Gerald fumed: "Dammit! One of those bitches is still wriggling!"

Charlene winced at the thought.

Gerald got out and Charlene heard more popping sounds. Gerald got back in; this time he was a more contented man.

"No more wriggling," he grinned.

Charlene sighed. He had killed them. They were really dead. She was sitting next to a murderer. What did that make her?

Six

"We're not animals!" shouted Gerald Gallego in the Placerville, California courtroom where he and his seven months pregnant wife, Charlene, appeared for a bail and arraignment hearing.

Both defendants entered pleas of not guilty to the charges against each of one count of kidnapping and one count of first-degree murder.

The judge ordered the defendants held without bail, pending a preliminary hearing, and remanded them back to the El Dorado County jail.

The case against the Gallegos had become a jurisdictional nightmare. Three Northern California jurisdictions were involved in the kidnap-murder of Craig Miller and Mary Beth Sowers. And the district attorneys from each of them wanted to put Gerald and Charlene Gallego on trial.

Miller and Sowers had initially been kidnapped from a shopping center in Sacramento. The body of Miller had been found in El Dorado County. An autopsy indicated that he had been shot to death at that location. Sowers's body was discovered in nearby Placer County. She too had been shot at the scene, according to the autopsy report.

El Dorado County District Attorney Ron Tepper appeared to be in the driver's seat amongst jurisdictions, since his county had begun the legal assault against the accused by charging Gerald and Charlene Gallego with the kidnapping and murder of Craig Miller. However, Tepper knew that the chances of successfully convicting the pair on the kidnap-murders of Miller and Sowers was very remote.

"You could have a theory that they [Gallegos] passed through our county and murdered Craig and then went on to Placer County," said Tepper, "or you could have a theory that they went to Placer County and did their deed over there and then brought him [Miller] back here and murdered him here. But I have no evidence of any sort of theory that she [Sowers] was ever in this county."

After conferring with the other respective district attorneys, it was jointly decided on November 25, 1980, that the Sacramento County District Attorney's office would prosecute the kidnap-murder case against Gerald and Charlene Gallego. It was the only practical way to proceed. Prosecuting the case in Sacramento County was based on the fact that the alleged abductions originated there. This would allow for the charges of multiple murders with special circumstances. Such circumstances were necessary under California law in order to impose the death penalty.

Furthermore, Sacramento County, with a population of nearly a million and a tax base relative to that, could certainly afford the burden of a potentially costly trial far better than its neighboring counties. Having the assistance of the California Department of Justice and the Sacramento County Crime Laboratory was a further plus in favor of the Sacramento County D.A.'s office.

The next step was to build a can't-lose case against Gerald Armond Gallego and Charlene Adell Gallego.

In the meantime, yet another Northern California county had become interested in the Gallegos in connection with a murder investigation. Yolo County investigators had been working on the unsolved murder of thirty-four-year-old Virginia Mochel since her body had been found on October 3, 1980, near Clarksburg in southeastern Yolo County. The West Sacramento bartender and mother of two had been missing since July 17, 1980, when she disappeared apparently after closing the Sail Inn tavern where she tended bar.

Shortly thereafter, detectives interviewed two patrons of the tavern that night, a Stephen Robert Feil and a woman claiming to be his girlfriend, who called herself Charlene Gallego. Both said they knew nothing about Mochel's disappearance, and they were not considered suspects from that point on.

The case had gone nowhere until it was revealed by Sacramento authorities that one of the suspects in the kidnap-murder of Craig Miller and presumed kidnapping of Mary Beth Sowers was a man named Gerald Armond Gallego, who went by the alias Stephen Robert Feil. His wife was identified as Charlene Gallego.

Detective David Trujillo of Yolo County had interviewed Feil, aka Gallego, or vice versa; and his wife, aka girlfriend, Charlene. In fact, he had interviewed her twice. He remembered that the couple had been driving a van when they went to the Sail Inn that night.

Given that the Gallegos had fled the state in an Oldsmobile, Trujillo set about searching for the van he believed might tie them conclusively with the abduction and murder of Virginia Mochel.

He tracked the van down in Orangevale, where the Gallegos had sold it to a couple in early August 1980. The couple turned over a blood-soaked sheet and mattress to Yolo County authorities, which they said came with the van. Carpet samples from the van were also retrieved by technicians and forwarded to the California Department of Justice Crime Lab for examination.

Although some of the "evidence" would be useful in helping solve the murders of Rhonda Scheffler and Kippi Vaught, it was insufficient to link the Gallegos directly to the slaying of Virginia Mochel.

Just as when Stephen Feil and Charlene Gallego were the initial suspects in Virginia Mochel's disappearance, they continued to stay a step or two ahead of the law in the investigation into her murder.

SEVEN

Two days after Kippi Vaught and Rhonda Martin Scheffler disappeared, migrant farm workers Aurelio Sanchez and Julio Martinez spotted the remains of two girls—or young women—it was hard to tell. They were lying in clumps of dead grass in a meadow near Sloughhouse, not far from the farm where the men worked.

By the time the Sacramento County Sheriff's Department received the call on the evening of September 13, 1978, stating that the bodies of two young females had been discovered, Gregory Scheffler, the nineteen-year-old husband of Rhonda Scheffler, had already put out the word that his wife was missing.

When Rhonda inexplicably left him waiting for a ride from her after work on the afternoon of Sep-

tember 11th, Gregory found it more than a little
odd. Rhonda was normally very dependable. His
first thought was that she and her friend Kippi had
lost track of the time during their visit to the Country Club Plaza, where the girls had gone to return
a pair of shoes.

But when he got home and realized neither
Rhonda nor her car were there, he sensed something other than tardiness was wrong. Gregory
phoned Kippi Vaught's mother, and the two eventually went to the Country Club Plaza in hopes
of finding a satisfactory answer to the missing girls.

As far as Mrs. Vaught was concerned, she could
think of no explanation that would be "satisfactory." She would later testify that "only an earth-
quake" could have prevented Rhonda from picking
up her husband as planned.

They located Rhonda's Vega in the parking lot,
but there was no sign of Rhonda or Kippi. Gregory
considered car trouble as the culprit until he put
his key in the ignition and it started right up. A
check of the trunk provided no clues, except for the
bags of merchandise the girls had purchased at the
mall.

Gregory and Kippi Vaught's mother then questioned store employees and anyone else who may
have had some knowledge about the missing two.
They came up empty.

By ten o'clock that night, a frustrated and fearful Gregory Scheffler decided it was time to report his wife and her friend to the sheriff's department as missing persons.

The following day, detectives learned from Kippi Vaught's mother that Kippi had run away from home in the past. This time, however, was unusual, said the mother, because as far as she could determine, none of her daughter's personal effects were missing. Rhonda and Kippi were said to be average students at a local high school, and both had attended school on September 11th.

Gregory enlisted the aid of the local media in the search for Rhonda and Kippi. Everyone wanted this case of missing persons to come to a happy conclusion.

It was not to be.

In spite of Gregory's apparent concern about his wife's absence, his possible involvement in it could not be dismissed by investigators. There was talk of heated arguments between the young married couple; Rhonda even had a life insurance policy for a modest amount. But, by most accounts, there was no evidence of serious marital problems or any pattern of behavior to indicate that Rhonda would ever walk away from her marriage. At least not voluntarily.

The bodies found near Sloughhouse were positively identified as seventeen-year-old Rhonda Martin Scheffler and sixteen-year-old Kippi Vaught.

According to the coroner, both girls had been sexually assaulted, bludgeoned, and shot to death. One of the victims had a bullet wound behind the left ear, the bullet grazing the skull. A second and fatal bullet was fired at close range into the back of the head. It has been speculated that this victim was the one to wiggle, catching Gerald Gallego's attention. Had she not, she may well have lived and identified her assailant and his co-conspirator before any others could be victimized. Regrettably, this would forever be left to speculation.

The first serious but erroneous lead in this case came on September 14th, when the police received a call from an unidentified young woman. She claimed she and three friends had seen the soon-to-be victims get into a red Pontiac Firebird that might have had out-of-state plates. The driver was identified as a black male. A second black male was also in the car, she told them, and provided descriptions of each.

The caller claimed to have known Rhonda and Kippi from high school. Reportedly one of the caller's pickup trucker friends, upon seeing Kippi and Rhonda enter the Firebird, had yelled: "Nigger lovers!"

A detective ultimately met with the "eyewitness" and her three friends—all of whom positively identified photographs of Kippi Vaught and Rhonda Scheffler.

Kippi Vaught did happen to know a young black man who worked for a boys' home. The extent of that relationship may never be known, but the young black man was soon to regret ever having been acquainted with Kippi.

The suspect was located. He owned a red Pontiac Firebird and matched the description provided by the alleged witness—neither of which helped his case.

It did not set well with authorities that he had been fired from his job due to drinking while on duty and setting a bad example for the boys he was supposed to be supervising.

Further damaging the young man's credibility and claims of innocence were inconsistencies in his statements to the police concerning his whereabouts the day Kippi Vaught and Rhonda Scheffler were killed. The police were soon able to track down another young black man, alleged to be the other person seen in the Firebird with Rhonda and Kippi.

The police now had not one, but two suspects. Clearly, prejudice had implicated the men from the start. Where this ended and solid investigative work began is something only the police would know for certain. Unfortunately for the suspects, being black and powerless, at a time when justice could not be served quickly enough for a hungry public, put them at a definite disadvantage.

The turn of events could not have worked out better for the real killers. As far as the world was concerned, Gerald and Charlene Gallego were just another average couple. Who could imagine that investigators could be so far off base? Worse yet was that the reign of terror by the two had only just begun.

After returning to their apartment from Sloughhouse, Gerald and Charlene went to bed as if they had just come back from a drive-in movie. Neither had much to say or, in Charlene's case, dared to say.

Realistically, what was there to say that had not already been said? The deed was done, and there was no way to undo it.

In the morning, the killers searched the victims' purses finding, among other things, paper for rolling marijuana cigarettes. Had they not been so paranoid about leaving evidence of the crime, the Gallegos might well have put the paper to good use.

Instead, they kept the contents of the purses intact, gathered up the clothes Gerald had worn the previous night, and the .25 caliber gun used on the victims, and left the apartment in the Oldsmobile to rid themselves of the incriminating items. A dumpster behind a clothing store would suffice for getting rid of the clothes.

Then they made their way to an area alongside the Sacramento River, where Charlene watched as Gerald put the .25 caliber pistol into one of the victim's purses, added a few rocks to further weigh it down, then flung the purse into the river. He put rocks and leaves into the other purse and tossed it into the water as well.

Unlocking the trunk, Gerald took out a tire iron. It had been used to bludgeon Kippi Vaught and Rhonda Scheffler. The stains from their blood coated one end. Charlene shuddered at the thought. What must it have been like for those poor girls? They probably, she rationalized, were better off dead.

Gerald held the bloody end of the tire iron up to her face and grinned. "You wanna touch it? Go ahead, it's dry."

She frowned at him and backed off. "That's not even funny, Gerry. Why don't you just get rid of the damned thing!"

He chuckled. "Good idea."

He hurled it as far as he could and they watched it splash into the river and vanish. Gerald checked the trunk once more before they considered this experience behind them and returned to the apartment.

*   *   *

Gerry insisted that Charlene have an abortion. There was no arguing with him whenever he made up his mind. Charlene had wanted to keep her baby. Or at least see it develop beyond two months into a real human being that could make, if not them, some lucky couple proud some day.

But it was not to be.

Still, she got brave and gave it one more try.

"Don't I have a say in this, Gerry?".

"Sure you do," he said grimly. "As long as it's the same as mine."

They entered the abortion clinic. At least, Charlene thought, I won't have to put up with this damned morning sickness any longer.

Gerald would see to that.

Charlene waited alongside others who had for one reason or another decided to terminate their pregnancies. When her name was finally called, she had a strong desire to run for the door. But she was sure Gerry would catch up and drag her back in.

So she went into the small yet intimidating room and tried to take her mind off what was about to happen. A brief thought about the girls Gerry had called his sex slaves was quickly replaced with thinking about how many more pregnancies she had left in her.

Once the procedure had been completed, Charlene was left alone to try and shake off the dizziness and nausea she was told were normal.

As far as Gerald was concerned, he had done them both a big favor.

After spending some time along the Oregon coast with friends, Gerald and Charlene stopped off in Chico on the return trip. Gerald's mother, Lorraine, lived there in a ranch house with her third—some believe fourth or fifth—husband, Ed Davies; Gerald's dear old and tough as nails grandmother; and his unnaturally beloved daughter, Krista.

If Gerald was expecting a warm reception, it was not forthcoming. It seemed as if his incestuous love for his daughter was now common knowledge in the family. In fact, Krista had gone one important step further. She had reported her father to the authorities.

Prompted by a classmate coming forward, Krista had told her story to Detective Sergeant Dan Young of the Butte County Sheriff's Office in a report dated September 27, 1978. She accused her father of sexually molesting her from the age of six until her current age of fourteen. The accusations included charges of incest, sodomy, oral copulation, and unlawful intercourse.

Detective Young, with a strong eye for a credible witness or victim, believed the young accuser. He had been prepared to arrest Gerald Gallego immediately, had he shown up.

But Gerald and Charlene were vacationing in Oregon at the time. Young strongly urged Lorraine Davies to notify him immediately should Gerald pay the family a visit.

Lorraine, who gave every indication of being shocked by the charges, would do as the detective suggested. She called the Butte County Sheriff's Office on September 28th upon seeing Gerald and his girlfriend drive up in the van.

Now she was trying to talk her son into giving up.

Charlene was genuinely shaken by Krista's accusations. Whether they were true or not—and she strongly suspected they were—how could Krista turn on Gerry like that? Whatever he may have done, believed Charlene, he truly loved his daughter—maybe even more than he did her.

Of less consideration to Charlene was the knowledge that this man she was trying to protect from charges of child molestation had recently raped, beaten, and murdered girls not much older than Krista. But that was not really very important. After all, this was a family matter.

"It's the best thing to do," Lorraine pleaded with her son. "You can get help."

Gerald actually thought about it. "Maybe you're right."

Charlene couldn't believe what she was hearing. He had murdered two girls. If he was arrested, he might never come out again. And what would happen to her?

Fate took another wrong turn, for before Gerald could carry through on his bluff, Lorraine's husband, Ed Davies, returned home from work.

The moment Ed, a short but strong-as-an-ox man, saw Gerald, his eyes lit with rage.

"You sonofabitch!" he cursed, and grabbed a rifle from the tool shed while shouting: "I'm gonna blow your damned head off!"

Gerald never gave him the chance. He grabbed Charlene, ran to the van, and sped off into the sunset.

EIGHT

If Charlene was more concerned about his facing
charges of lewd and lascivious conduct with his
daughter, Gerald was far more interested in protecting himself in the event that his and Charlene's
secret sex slave experience came to light. He had
been behind bars enough to know that he never
wanted to see the inside of a jail or prison cell
again. He also knew a bit about death row and
execution, thanks in part to good old dad.

Gerald was determined not to follow suit, especially in being betrayed by his accomplice. Although he trusted Charlene, he knew full well trust
could be bought and sold if the price was right. The
way he saw it, he would either have to eventually
kill Charlene to keep her quiet—or marry her.

The second option seemed more appropriate for the time being.

Gerald Armond Gallego and Charlene Adell Williams were married in Reno on September 30, 1978. It was number six for him, three for her. They would each add one more, unofficially, before it was over.

In attendance, acting as witnesses, were Charlene's parents, Charles and Mercedes Williams. They must have thought their pride and joy, Charlene, was finally to have that storybook romance she had wanted all her life.

If only they had known just what their dear daughter had gotten herself into.

From Gerald's viewpoint, it was not enough to have Charlene as his wife to act as a safeguard. What he also needed was a new name to throw those Butte County Sheriff assholes off stride, and Charlene would help him do it.

He picked out a name in her family lineage—Stephen Robert Feil—a distant relative whom he had no idea was a California state cop. It was up to Charlene to convince mommy and daddy that they needed this fake birth certificate in order to start the marriage off on the right track. Besides, Charlene convinced them as only she could, Gerry was innocent of the charges that he had molested his daughter and her fourteen-year-old girlfriend.

Charles and Mercedes bought it hook, line, and sinker . . .

Gerald Armond Gallego was now officially Stephen Robert Feil—when it suited his purposes.

The name change did not come soon enough. On October 9, 1978, an arrest warrant was issued for Gallego. The felony offenses included incest, sodomy, and oral copulation. Bail was set at $50,000.

Gerald decided that getting out of town for a while was his best move. He and Charlene packed up a few belongings and headed to Houston, where Charles Williams used his network of connections to line up a job for Gerald.

Unfortunately, it lasted only briefly after Gerald and his supervisor failed to see eye to eye.

In early December of 1978, Gerald Gallego, aka Stephen Feil, took a job as a bartender at a place called Whiskey Junction, a popular Houston nightclub. For the three months Gallego held on to this job, Charlene spent much of the time alone and lonely at their apartment. No doubt she had all but blocked out of her mind the horrors she and Gerry had perpetrated on those innocent girls seemingly so long ago.

Her greatest thoughts now were for stability and doing what she could to make Gerald happy. That did not include working. He had a problem with her working at even the most menial of jobs. Somehow this made him believe she was challenging his authority. Not to mention his insecurity, when it came to her intelligence. It was no big deal to Charlene that she had more on the ball upstairs than Gerry. Lots of wives were smarter than their husbands.

She would give up a few points off her IQ to become the number one girl with heart. She suspected she was not at the moment.

By March of 1979, Gerald Gallego alias Stephen Feil was up to his old tricks when it came to his renowned temper. A dispute at Whiskey Junction with a fellow bartender turned into a brawl.

"He [Stephen Feil] beat the all-fired hell out of this bartender," said the club's bookkeeper. "I called them down, talked to them. I think it was the very next night he [Stephen] came in and turned in his resignation. He said he couldn't work with the guy anymore."

Apparently Gallego had tired of Houston as well. He and Charlene ended up in Reno before the year was out. Once again, Charles Williams came to the rescue. He got Gerald a job driving a truck for a meat plant. The manager said Williams introduced Gallego as "Stephen Feil, his son-in-law." Home for the Gallegos became a rented condominium in nearby Sparks.

In April of 1979, Charlene added to the income

by going to work for another meat company as a receptionist and sales representative. It was hardly what she had in mind during her promising days in grade school. She had considered herself a chip off her daddy's block when it came to eventual success in the business world.

But that was before she met Gerry and was forced to more or less abandon her ideas of liberation, success, equality. The man was in charge, Gerry would tell her; the woman did what she was told.

Things were not going particularly well in the bedroom either these days. Gerald's continual problems and pressures on the job put added strain on their sex life. Not that it wasn't already strained. Gerry often could not get an erection and Charlene was usually blamed for it. She either was too fat, too skinny, too lousy in bed, or unwilling to do any and everything he wanted her to do to satisfy him.

Sometimes he would force her to try new positions, old positions, unnatural acts . . . Other times she would be creative in trying to please him. More often than not, Charlene was incapable of satisfying a man who did not know the meaning of the word.

Gerald Gallego aka Stephen Feil's job as a truck driver lasted just over a month. "He [Gallego] and my foreman got into a disagreement," the manager recalled, "and he [Gallego] walked out."

73

Charlene, fearful of what could happen if Gerald was unemployed, bored, restless, and had too much time to think, begged the manager to allow him to stay on. The manager refused.

Father's Day in 1979 fell on June 24th. In Reno, it also happened to be a day when the Washoe County Fair was going full steam, with the locals taking the spotlight over the thousands of tourists who flocked daily to the biggest little gambling town in the world. Young girls could be seen in adult bodies, tight shorts, and budding breasts beneath halter tops and body hugging T-shirts.

For two such girls this would be the last Father's Day they would ever see.

At the same time, another girl had narrowly averted a similar fate. Gerald Gallego had set his sights on a twelve-year-old girl that happened to be the daughter of friends of Charlene's parents, who lived in Sparks. Charlene, not quite as cold-blooded as her husband, used her best persuasive powers to steer Gerry clear of that innocent little girl.

"You're right," he rationalized, "bad idea. It might point to us."

Unfortunately, in Gerald's mind, that meant someone else had to take her place. He informed Charlene that the spirit of his sex slave fantasy once again moved him. It was time to find some live bait.

74

For Charlene, this had to be expected sooner or later. Even though they had not talked about the first two victims in some time, it was a given that Gerry would not want to leave it at that. Particularly with the finger of blame pointed at those black guys. As far as Gerald Gallego was concerned, he and Charlene were in the free and clear to add to his list of young, fresh sexual slaves to do his bidding.

The next victims would also be easy, with plenty of others around to take the blame. That's the good old-fashioned American system of justice for you. Imperfect. Prejudiced. Brain dead.

Besides, Charlene knew, Gerry's sex drive had all but stalled with her. This was his way of regenerating, and she had better not argue the point. After all, she was in this as deeply as him and always would be, she decided, for better or worse.

Gerald and Charlene had been cruising the streets of Reno in their van looking for potential victims before arriving at the Washoe County Fairgrounds. There were more girls there than Gerald could count. The trick was to pick out the ripe and ready ones.

He went over the plan once again with Charlene. She was to pretend to be looking for people to distribute handbills on automobile windshields. Get the girls over to the van, he told Charlene, and I'll take over from there.

Once more, Charlene became the innocuous-appearing lure for some unsuspecting, naive, soon-to-be victims. She went off on her search, almost comfortable in her adept skill at smooth talking and avoiding undue suspicion. If she had any second thoughts about her role in this insanity, Charlene successfully suppressed them well in the back of her mind, out of reach of her conscience.

Armed with a .38 caliber revolver Gerry had given her—just in case—Charlene felt its weight in her purse. She wondered if she would ever have the nerve to use it? The thought of actually shooting someone made her shiver.

She knew full well that was not the case with Gerry. He had left no doubt of his callous willingness to pull the trigger when he gunned down those last two girls. He carried a .44 caliber over-and-under derringer in his jacket pocket, and would not hesitate to use it—especially if he felt cornered like a rat.

Charlene appeared for all the world to seem like a sweet, pretty, fair-goer who would make a good companion for the many young men whose path she had likely crossed as she strolled about haphazardly. Few could have believed that such a potentially good catch could actually be there all by her lonesome.

Their instincts could not have been more right.

Charlene had a job to do and she took it seriously. Trouble was, she had yet to come upon one, let alone two or three girls, who were pretty, thin, spacey, and without male companionship. There was no sense in bringing someone that Gerry would not like. All he would do is take it out on her later.

Charlene, careful to avoid suspicion, had gone the length of the fair and back without finding the right girls. Then she saw them. Two girls about to exit the fairgrounds. They were perfect.

Brenda Lynne Judd, fourteen, and Sandra Kay Colley, thirteen, typified most young girls who came to the fair primarily to see and be seen. They were at the age where boys meant just about everything. But first you had to be able to attract them. Both girls had little problem in that department. Cute, streetwise, precocious. One had the slender, long blonde-haired look; the other was more petite, with short, curly, raven hair.

They'd had fun all day and were to meet a friend by the entrance for the ride home. The girls were all giggles as they noticed the young woman approaching them. It would never have occurred to them that she represented danger. How could she? She didn't look the part.

Besides, she had handbills in her hand. She was obviously looking for volunteers.

"If you girls want to make a few bucks," Charlene said nonchalantly, "all you have to do is stick

these"—she held up a handbill—"on car windshields."

The girls looked at each other. Why not? they
thought. Money was money, and there never
seemed to be enough. They had a little bit of time
before their ride came. Why not make good use of
it?

"Okay," the girls said in unison.

They followed the small woman to a van, hardly
noticing the man approaching from another angle.
When they did notice him, it was too late. He had
the .44 pointed at their faces.

"Care to go for a little ride?" Gerald grinned.

The Gallegos had added a mattress to the back
of the van since the last sex slaves. Gerald forced
his two captives to lie face down on the mattress
that was covered by two thin blankets. He then
bound them, hand and foot, and the real terror was
about to begin.

Charlene sat in the back with the frightened,
whimpering girls while Gerald drove the van out
of the fairgrounds and away from the captives' best
hope for help.

"Everything will be okay," Charlene made herself say to the girls, as if she really believed it. She
said it again, though with much less conviction.

She knew undoubtedly that Gerry was not going
to have his way with the girls and let them live to
tell someone, maybe the cops, about it. Yet Char-

lene felt some compassion for them as human beings, and as vulnerable females. She knew something about that. In many ways, she was as vulnerable as them. She knew Gerry's secrets but could tell no one.

Maybe someday, it occurred to Charlene, as if for the first time, he would kill her too.

Gerald stopped off at a building supply store, leaving Charlene and his sex slaves alone inside the van. So confident was he of his hold over his wife and domination over his petrified captives, Gerald had little fear they would try to make a run for it. Least of all, Charlene. If she was going to try anything suicidal like that, he reasoned, she would have already done so.

Gerald returned to the van, having purchased a sparkling silver-bladed shovel and hammer. They were off again on a journey of no return for two of the van's occupants.

They drove onto Interstate 80 and headed east. One girl became physically ill during the bumpy ride; the other suffered just as greatly mentally. There was little Charlene could do to comfort them other than offer false assurances.

At some point during the drive, Gerald had Charlene trade places with him. It did not take Charlene long to realize that this time Gerry planned to perpetrate his sex slave fantasy in her presence.

She heard him order the girls to undress. Charlene peeked in the rearview mirror at the goings-on in the back. She could see the girls remove what little clothing they wore.

Then they, and Gerry, were down on the mattress, out of her sight. Thank goodness, Charlene thought. The last thing she needed was to see Gerry having sex with two other women. That was between him and them.

Dusk turned to dark as Charlene continued the drive to nowhere for what must have seemed like an eternity, while Gerry violated and abused his slaves. She could hear the girls crying, moaning, and breathing. Similar sounds, oddly enough to her, came from Gerry.

"Slow this damned thing down," ordered Gerald hotly when he sensed Charlene was going too fast.

She lifted her foot off the accelerator. "Sorry," she murmured, more to herself. "It's hard to keep it at fifty-five when there's nothing but endless road and darkness before you."

Gerald must have decided that her driving might get them in trouble, so he took over the wheel. "Keep your eyes on those two," he spat, shoving Charlene in the back. "I hope to hell you can at least do that right."

Charlene got a bird's-eye view of the raped, exhausted, scared victims. If she put herself in their shoes, it was for but a fleeting moment. She could not afford to be sympathetic. Had she been, it would probably drive her crazy. There was really nothing she could do for them, Charlene thought, but hope perhaps that Gerry might dump them in the desert and give them at least a fighting chance for survival.

They finally stopped somewhere in the high Nevada desert and Gerald took off with one of his captives, leaving Charlene alone with the other. What the hell was she to say to her? Charlene wondered. You are going to die for your trouble?

She chose to remain speechless. No chance she could let the girl go. If I did, thought Charlene sincerely, it would be me to take her place out there.

Gerald returned to the van alone. Charlene had heard no shots this time. She knew he had weapons with him just as capable—his new shovel and hammer.

"Let's go, bitch!" he yelled at the remaining victim.

Weak and powerless, she did little to resist her brutal and frightening captor. One could imagine, though, her taking one last desperate look at Charlene, a woman not much older than her, and thinking: Why are you letting him do this? What did we ever do to you to deserve to be raped and murdered?

Charlene would not have been able to justify her own actions and inactions. She watched, almost turning a blind eye, while Gerald dragged the girl into the darkness of the desert. Moments later, he returned with the hammer and shovel.

"Are they dead?" asked Charlene meekly.

"What the hell do you think?" growled Gerald, as if to say, use your head for once, Charlene. You're the one that's supposed to be so damned smart. What other choice did I have?

Gerald drove and Charlene took a final look at the death scene, what little she could see. Neither of them realized she would later try, unsuccessfully, to find it again, this time with anxious police investigators by her side.

Right now, Charlene's thoughts were on trying to put behind her the latest episode in Gerry's sex slave fantasy. When would it stop? she wondered. How many more would there be?

Would she ever be enough for him?

NINE

Gerald Armond Gallego, Jr. was born on January 17, 1981, in a hospital prison ward. Charlene Gallego, twenty-four was forced to witness the birth of her child while in custody as an alleged kidnapper and murderess. Her husband, Gerald, thirty-four and co-accused, was also detained and unable to see his child come into the world.

It is doubtful that Gerald Gallego, who had forced his wife to have an abortion several years earlier, and who probably had more kids than he could count, cared that his namesake had survived nine months of hell. Gerald was too busy trying to find ways to save his own neck and make certain Charlene was not the one to chop it off.

Charlene, on the other hand, likely had some misgivings that her child had to be born this way.

She counted on her parents to give him the same good home she had. If she was lucky, she would get to join Gerry, Jr., very soon.

It was a good thing she did not make plans to be present when he celebrated his first birthday or, for that matter, at least the next fifteen birthdays.

The entire year of 1981 proved to be a frustrating one for both the Gallegos and those who would try to put them away for a very long time.

In early January 1981, at the request of the Gallegos, a preliminary hearing was held in the Sacramento Municipal Court before Judge Peter Mering. Charlene, represented by a family attorney, was requesting bail on the grounds that a refusal to grant such "violated the rights of her unborn child."

The attorney wrote in a motion: "There can be no argument that the fetus within Charlene is not guilty of any wrongdoing. That fetus, and the innocent child which will be born, should not be punished . . . by keeping Charlene in custody, the child is being punished."

Judge Mering denied the motion, stating that bail for Charlene Gallego would only be considered if the defense could provide "evidence or affidavits" that contradicted the prosecutors' case against Charlene.

Meanwhile, both Charlene's attorney and Gerald Gallego's public defender called for a discovery hearing in order to determine if there was sufficient evidence to link the Gallegos to the kidnap-murders of Craig Miller and Mary Beth Sowers.

The request was based on another double kidnapping and murder case that occurred after the Gallegos were in custody. On December 21, 1980, University of California Davis students John Harrold Riggins and Sabrina Marie Gonsalves, both eighteen, were abducted near the campus. Two days later their bodies, throats slashed, were found in Sacramento County. The defense motion stated that "the similarities could be taken to infer that the perpetrators of the UC Davis homicide also committed the [California State University, Sacramento] homicides."

The common themes between the Miller-Sowers murders and Riggins-Gonsalves murders were interesting, to say the least. Were the timing and circumstances merely coincidence? Or an attempt to let Gerald and Charlene Gallego off the hook by calling their alleged kidnapping-murder of Miller and Sowers into question?

There is reason to believe the latter was true. On November 13, 1989, Gerald Gallego's half-brother, David Raymond Hunt; Hunt's wife, Sue Ellen; and an ex-cellmate, Richard Thompson, were arrested and charged by law enforcement officers in Woodland, California with the copycat kidnapping-murders of Riggins and Gonsalves. Although the outcome of this case is unknown, the implications and possibilities continue to be intriguing.

However, back in January of 1981, the Gonsalves-Riggins murders did not help win the release of Gerald or Charlene Gallego. Nor would they ever.

In another ironic twist involving Gallego's half-brother, David Hunt, and ex-cellmate, Richard Thompson, it was widely believed by law enforcement authorities that Hunt and Thompson were involved in a plot to help the Gallegos escape during the hearing or trial. This led to increased security at the hearing, metal detectors, and general hysteria.

No attempt to escape was made—perhaps due to the added precautions.

During the hearing, the defense also challenged the testimony of the fraternity brother who had written down the license number of Charlene Gallego's Oldsmobile, which had proved to be the break needed to end the Gallegos' reign of kidnapping, rape, and murder. It was argued that when the authorities hypnotized the fraternity brother during their investigation, this made him an unreliable, non-credible witness.

The judge disagreed, doubting that the fraternity brother had "really" been hypnotized and, therefore, his testimony would still stand. At least for the time being.

Gerald and Charlene Gallego were to remain held for the kidnap and murder of Craig Miller and Mary Beth Sowers.

In July of 1981, Charlene Gallego was beginning to show her first signs of breaking away from—and ultimately betraying—her domineering husband and his hold on her. While still represented by her parents' attorney, Charlene contacted the D.A.'s office and promised cooperation in exchange for having bail set and her release from custody.

Her allegations were that she knew nothing about the Sowers-Miller murders. She claimed that they were still alive when Gerald drove off with the couple from his apartment. He returned alone. Only then did Charlene notice blood on his jacket.

The prosecution did not buy into this lie. They were determined to try both Gallegos in this double kidnapping and murder. Unless, of course, there was a development that was too much for them to ignore.

Charlene was giving this much thought.

TEN

Sandra Colley and Brenda Judd were not waiting by the entrance of the Washoe County Fair as their friend had expected on that Father's Day, June 24, 1979. The friend had only missed the pair by minutes. Not realizing they were nowhere to be found, the friend searched the fairgrounds in vain.

That evening, she finally reported Colley and Judd as missing to the Reno Police Department. As was usually the case when teenagers disappear, the first thought to arise was that they ran away. There are millions of runaways and throwaways every year, often inexplicable to those who thought they knew them best. Why was this any different?

For one, according to family and friends, neither girl had a history of running away, substance abuse, or incorrigible behavior. If there were any severe problems at home, no one seemed to know about it.

This was enough to at least convince the Reno police to take the disappearance seriously enough to look into it. They searched the city for the girls, interviewed fairground employees and attendees and, in short, went through the normal, if not excessive, procedures of trying to locate missing persons.

One story emerged that two girls fitting Judd and Colley's descriptions had run away with the carnival that had lent its games and rides to the county fair. Reno police followed this lead, and the carnival, which was now in Salt Lake City. Two Reno girls had in fact joined the carnival as runaways. Unfortunately, they were not Brenda Judd or Sandra Colley.

Other leads eventually had investigators making inquiries in California, Oregon, and Washington—to no avail.

If the Reno police suspected kidnapping or murder, this was never relayed to the girls' families. There was no indication this had been the case. Likely, the police regarded the missing girls as runaways, until proven otherwise.

Once again, the killers had been aided and abetted by circumstances and luck. Like the victims before them, Brenda Judd and Sandra Colley were unable to lead the police in the right direction. Nor were they ever going to.

As had become habit after Gerald Gallego's sex slave fantasy was completed, Charlene cleaned the van so that it was almost as good as new, inside and out. No one would ever expect that they had used it to kidnap, assault, and murder four young girls.

Actually, Gerry had done it, thought Charlene. She refused to take blame for his actions. Anyone could have lured them. But not everyone—certainly not her—could do what he did to those girls and be able to sleep at night.

Gerry seemed to have no problem doing that. Except when he wanted her as his sex slave. He expected and demanded that Charlene be his whore. Whether he wanted masturbation, oral sex, vaginal sex, anal sex or something even more kinky, it was up to her to satisfy him. Never mind about satisfying her.

Charlene had more or less given up on that. Gerry didn't believe it was his place to please her in bed. If she wanted to be pleased, she had to do it herself.

Not that there weren't other men around. There had always been other men—like the married man Charlene had been seeing before Gerry came along and turned her attentions elsewhere.

Then there was her current boss, the sales manager. She could always tell when a man was attracted to her, even before he could. She liked her boss. He was good looking and nice to her.

She could easily have seduced him or vice versa. But she could not allow that to happen. Not even if life with Gerry was becoming more and more strained and less and less fulfilling.

She did not want to cause trouble for the man. And trouble was just what he would get if he tried to come between her and Gerry.

Gerry was extremely possessive and jealous. Charlene knew that to ignite these weaknesses could cost her sales manager his life. And maybe hers as well.

On July 2, 1979, Gerald, as Stephen Feil, went to work as a driver for a soft drink bottling company in Reno. Meanwhile, his problems with Charlene continued in and out of the bedroom. She had become a "whiner" to him. What he wanted was someone who could take the heat, someone he could count on when the going got rough. And it probably would, when all was said and done.

He also wanted someone who could rid him of his damned impotence. Charlene lacked the heart and sexual skills for that lofty mission.

What the hell use was she anyway? he began to wonder.

Gerald and Charlene quit their jobs in early September of 1979 and returned to Sacramento. Charlene's co-workers were not unhappy to see her leave as she was accused of "often losing her temper" and using "abusive language."

Obviously it was catching.

Mindful of the Chico warrant against him, Gerald continued to use his new name, Stephen Feil, in Sacramento. He and Charlene were Mr. and Mrs. Stephen Feil as they moved into an apartment on Woodhollow Way in early October 1979.

For the next three months, Gerald worked off and on as a truck driver. Even when money was tight, Charlene had the luxury of knowing that any needed funds were just a phone call away to her parents, Charles and Mercedes Williams. Charlene was not afraid to abuse her privilege.

During this time, Gerald began to amass a collection of weapons, including a .357 Magnum Colt Python, a .38 revolver, an AR-15 rifle, and his over-and-under derringer. Soon he would add a .25 caliber handgun that would prove to be a fatal error in judgement.

Gerald applied for and received a California driver's license as Stephen Robert Feil. Perhaps in Gallego's mind this made it official and, therefore, put him out of reach of the law.

A few days before Christmas in 1979, Gerald as Stephen Feil got a job as a bartender at the Bob-Les

Club on Del Paso Boulevard.

The club's manager noted that Gallego did his job well. His one complaint was that Gallego was "quite an operator—quite a ladies' man."

This could account for why Gerald chose to introduce Charlene as his girlfriend rather than wife. It was common knowledge among club employees and patrons that Gerald was regularly seeing other women at this time. One such woman, Patty, would later tell investigators that she was expecting Gerald's child.

Patty probably saw in Gerald what Charlene had initially: a man that could be kind, considerate, affectionate, romantic. She could not have known him as the murderous sex maniac he was. And this may have saved her life.

Gerald eventually told Patty that he was married. By that time, he had her wrapped around his finger—just like Charlene. Only the bond could never be as tight between them. Charlene knew too much for anyone to ever take her place outright.

But Patty was a pleasant diversion for Gerald. After all, she knew how to please him in bed in ways Charlene could not even imagine. The perfect cure for his impotence. How long it would last was anybody's guess.

He would keep it going as long as she kept him happy and satisfied. What Charlene didn't know wouldn't hurt her.

Whether she knew or not was debatable. Chances are Charlene would have preferred Gerald's passionate affair with Patty to his sadistic, murderous, sex fantasy ritual with unwilling young girls.

In any event, thought Charlene, if Gerry was preoccupied sexually, maybe he would leave her alone. She could take sex or leave it these days. Mostly she could leave it.

What Charlene could not leave was the physical abuse she took from Gerald whenever it suited his fancy and mood. Almost anything could set him off without warning. She fought back from time to time, but was no match for her muscular brute of a husband.

Leaving him was out of the question for Charlene. She doubted he would ever let her go. Sure they would split up from time to time. He liked having his space whenever he accused her of cramping his style.

Inevitably, they would get back together. Charlene imagined it would always be this way. She and Gerry were forever bound, till death do they part.

On March 28, 1980, Charlene purchased, at Gerald's request, a second .25 caliber automatic pistol at a Sacramento sporting goods store on Arden Way. The .25 caliber Beretta was, unknowingly to the couple, the beginning of the end for their murderous spree.

But not before they added to their collection of bodies.

ELEVEN

"I want a girl!" spat Gerald at Charlene on the morning of April 24, 1980.

Charlene, adjusting her eyes to the sun rays seeping through the blinds in their bedroom, knew exactly what he meant. If his voice did not tell her, the cold hunger of his eyes did.

It had been exactly ten months since Brenda Judd and Sandra Colley had been abducted, sexually assaulted, and beaten to death. Charlene had nearly disassociated herself from it.

Now Gerry wanted to put her through this all over again. Not to mention some new, helpless victims.

"Get up!" demanded Gerald. "The sooner we get this over with, the sooner we can both get some sleep, or whatever—"

Charlene dragged herself out of bed. There was simply no escaping Gerry's warped sexual urges. If he said he wanted to do something—they did it.

She should have seen it coming, Charlene thought while getting dressed. Yesterday they had played softball and gone for a drink afterwards. Inexplicably, Gerry had become livid and they left the bar. She never knew what to expect from him from moment to moment, let alone day to day.

This was underscored when during breakfast, Gerald threw his breakfast, plate and all, on the floor. When Charlene tried to pick it up, he shouted at her: "Leave it! We've got more important things to do."

Before they left, Gerald took a white macrame rope from the closet by the front door. He cut several feet of rope and stuffed it in his pocket. Charlene was also aware that he had his .357 Magnum revolver with him.

Driving the van, the two began scouting for the perfect sex slaves. The search took them to a convenience store, a record store, a high school, and, ironically, Country Club Plaza where the killing spree had begun a year and a half earlier with the abduction of Kippi Vaught and Rhonda Scheffler.

Gerald and Charlene could not agree on any of the locations, before they ended up at Sunrise Mall. The mall was located in Citrus Heights, a growing suburban city just outside of Sacramento. Two decades earlier the mall was still a developer's dream. It replaced what had been rural country with farms, weeds, open land, cows, and horses.

Now the Sunrise Mall was in full bloom and had the distinction of being the largest indoor mall in Sacramento County. When coupled with the outdoor Birdcage Mall directly across the street, shoppers came from throughout the county to browse and spend.

The Gallegos had a far more ominous purpose in mind. They parked near one of several entrances to the mall and, like before, Gerald went over instructions for his dominated wife and willing accomplice.

This time, give them the marijuana line again, he told her. Kids fall for it every time. They think the stuff makes them grown. Instead, he chuckled while staying grim-faced, it stunts their growth.

Charlene and Gerald entered the mall. It was not unusually crowded, but still had a healthy supply of young, scantily clad bodies.

"There." directed Gerald. With his eyes, he pointed at two girls emerging from a bookstore.

Charlene saw them. They could not have been more than fifteen or sixteen. They looked as if they were lost, or at least undecided where to go from there.

That indecisiveness was to be their undoing.

* * *

Karen Chipman Twiggs and Stacy Ann Redican, both seventeen, had recently gotten jobs at a fast food restaurant. They had decided to spend some of their first paycheck at the mall as well as just hang out. The girls were about ready to leave when a blonde-haired woman literally stepped in front of them.

"You girls like smoking dope?" she asked them evenly.

"Yeah," said the brunette one eagerly. "Doesn't everybody?"

The blonde woman grinned. "Certainly everyone I know."

"You have some?" asked the other girl, her long, blonde hair more golden than the one she was speaking to.

"Do I ever." Charlene gave them her most friendly smile. "Come with me."

They did. The three headed out of the mall, passing by a man who gave little indication of interest in them. They could not have been more mistaken.

Charlene led her captives into the back of the van. Almost embarrassingly, she told them: "There is no dope here."

The girls glanced at each other with puzzled looks.

"You're wrong," the voice boomed at the back doors. The girls turned. "There are two dopes here."

And he pointed his .357 Magnum at them to back him up.

"You girls are being kidnapped," Gerald said matter-of-factly, as he climbed in the back. "As long as you do what you're told, you won't be hurt."

Interestingly enough, it seemed to be this fear of being hurt that allowed Gallego to control all of his victims with almost no resistance until, of course, it was too late.

Charlene drove east on Interstate 80. She wondered where the gravesite would be for these latest slaves. Why did they always come with her? she could not help but ask herself. Did anyone ever ask questions anymore of a total stranger? Was she really that trustworthy to the naked eye?

Gerry ordered his sex slaves to strip. Charlene watched off and on through the rearview mirror as the girls removed their clothing. Their bodies, taut and shapely, breasts full and round, almost made Charlene jealous with envy.

She knew that Gerald was always comparing his sex slaves' bodies with hers. And she never measured up. Any imperfections she had were something he not only found but ridiculed. Why couldn't she look like other girls, he would tell her, girls with heart and a tight ass!

Peeking through the mirror while Gerry sexually violated his slaves, Charlene could not help but think: Why should I be jealous? Whatever they had that she didn't, at least she would live through the day.

She doubted very much they could say the same.

Charlene cruised past Truckee and into the Sierras. Reaching Reno in the quickly approaching dark of night, one captive boasted about once living there. Perhaps she did not realize the severity of the situation? Or maybe it was her way of coping with what had to be her worst nightmare.

Gerald told Charlene to pull off the interstate, where they stopped at a supermarket. He bound the girls' hands behind their backs with the rope from the macrame, and left. He returned shortly thereafter with cigarettes and a new hammer.

Charlene silently resumed driving through the night desert, beyond Sparks, the West Humboldt Range, the Trinity Range, before approaching Lovelock, some ninety miles away from the glittering casinos of Reno. Earlier, they had passed Baxter, the place where Gerald's first sex slaves had been sexually assaulted. Charlene wondered if they would end up convicting those black men for the murder of those two girls?

The sexual assault continued and Gerald enjoyed every minute of it. He felt powerful against the powerless. They were completely under his domination and there was not a damned thing they could do about it.

Following Gerald's directions, Charlene drove through the darkness to Limerick Canyon, an area near Lovelock, Nevada where she and Gerry had once gone camping with friends.

She parked the van while Gerald lit a lantern.

"Hey," he said to her, "you want these girls? I think they're your type!"

She was not tempted in the slightest. Having sex with girls against their will was not her idea of sexual satisfaction.

She told Gerry, "Thanks but no thanks."

He looked disappointed, she thought oddly.

Gerald got out of the van. He was polite to his victims, almost to a fault, considering what he had just done—and intended to do.

"I'm just going to fix up a place for us to spend the night," he told them.

They wanted to take him at his word as he left his bound slaves and Charlene to wander out into the darkness. Only Charlene knew for a fact that Gerald's promises were about as phony as nearly everything else about him.

"Is he going to kill us?" asked the one who seemed to speak for both of them, when there was any conversation at all.

"No," lied Charlene mechanically. "Everything will be just fine. You'll see."

Gerald returned. He grabbed the green-handled,

fold-up shovel he had recently purchased, and the hammer.

"You!" he pointed at the spokesgirl. "Let's go."

He favored the other girl grimly, then faced Charlene and said tersely: "Watch her!" He handed Charlene the .357 Magnum.

Gerald led his sex slave away and Charlene watched with both awkwardness and detachment. After doing this so many times, there seemed no room left for pity or regret. Just get it over with and pretend it never happened.

Gerald came back alone and took the second girl away, carrying his tools of torture and death.

Once again Gerald returned without the one he left with. "Come take a look, Charlene," he said eagerly. "See where the girls are."

"I'd really rather not," she stammered. Somehow never seeing the corpses made the whole situation more digestible.

"I'd really rather you did!" blared Gerald tartly.

Charlene knew she had no choice. He would make her see what he had done to those girls. She imagined him using the hammer . . . shovel . . .

She followed him, almost blindly, in the night. It was eerily quiet. Almost too quiet. There were two graves, Charlene saw. Her eyes were aghast. She thought she saw something move.

"Don't worry," laughed Gerald, "they're good and dead."

He had a piece of tree branch that he used to smooth the ground with over the graves.

"Can we go now, Gerry?" sighed Charlene. She had seen enough. Why torture her with his handiwork?

He laughed. "If you insist."

Back at the van, Gerald ordered her to start cleaning it immediately. "Be sure to wipe everything," he insisted. She complied obediently. Nothing could tie them to this. Nothing.

There were six of them now. If anyone ever found out, she and Gerry would probably face the gas chamber. Or was it the electric chair?

They drove back towards Interstate 80. Charlene waited until her instincts told her what her eyes could not see in the darkness: that this was the perfect spot to get rid of the evidence. She threw the hammer out the window with as much strength as she could muster.

TWELVE

Charlene was in a mood to talk. After spending more than a year behind bars and deciding that her husband, Gerald, could neither hurt nor help her, now seemed the time to try and help herself.

The first thing had been to get rid of the attorney who, as far as she was concerned, was not qualified to handle a criminal defense. Certainly not hers, with so much at stake. So she contacted the superior court judge whom she was advised could help her.

In February 1982, Charlene Gallego was appointed two replacement attorneys, Hamilton Hintz, Jr. and Fern Laethem, to handle her case or, in her mind, get her off the hook. After all, she was not really guilty of anything except maybe naivety. If anyone deserved blame for what happened to those people, it was Gerry—and Gerry alone.

"What can you do to get me out of this mess?" Charlene asked her new attorneys.

"What can you do, Charlene, to get yourself out of this mess?"

Swallowing the lump in her throat, Charlene took a moment or two. For she knew that what she was about to reveal would effectively end whatever there was that existed between her and Gerry. Starting with the trust he counted on.

But that was before he got stupid with Craig Miller and Mary Beth Sowers and allowed them to be discovered and apprehended. Gerry deserved whatever he got for not being able to better control his sex fantasies and drinking.

Besides, she now had his son to think about.

Charlene looked at her attorneys and said: "We're not just talking about two kidnappings and murders here." She had caught their attention with a dramatic pause. Good. It was now or never. She chose now. Sorry, Gerry. "Try ten—"

She may have fallen short by one—Linda Aguilar's unborn child—but she had clearly made her point.

Charlene watched almost amusingly as her attorneys stared at each other, then her, speechless.

Before Charlene Gallego could tell her tale of sexual slavery and serial killings, the prosecution was

108

attempting to build its case against Charlene and Gerald Gallego for the kidnapping-murder of Craig Miller and Mary Beth Sowers. Deputy District Attorney James Morris would prosecute the case when and if it ever went to trial. That was never a given, no matter how despicable the crime and disliked the accused. There had to be sufficient evidence, withstanding legal challenges by the defense, and sincere belief by the prosecution that there was a good—make that great—chance for a conviction.

Complicating this particular case was the lack of a real motive, the multiple jurisdictions in which the crime had occurred, and eventually the bombshell dropped by one of the suspects that would shake the system to its foundation.

For now, everything appeared to be on the right track in the pretrial investigation. Frank Dale, investigator for the Sacramento County District Attorney's office, was to spearhead the prosecution's investigative team in establishing the case against the Gallegos.

Perhaps the most damaging evidence against Gerald Gallego, in particular, was the bullets that killed Craig Miller. Ballistics tests showed that they were a positive match with bullets taken from the ceiling of the Bob-Les bar. Those bullets were fired into the ceiling in the spring of 1980 by Gerald Gallego, aka Stephen Feil, during a "macho" demonstration characteristic of Gallego. At the time, he was a bartender at the bar and was seeking to impress a young woman.

The impression Gallego made on her would cost him dearly half a year later. For it was that woman who—after hearing of Gerald Gallego alias Stephen Feil being suspected of murdering Mary Beth Sowers and Craig Miller—remembered Gallego firing the shots into the ceiling. She contacted police with this vital information.

The California Department of Justice Crime Laboratory confirmed the suspicions of detectives. The bullets from the ceiling of the bar were a ballistics match with those that had been fired into Craig Miller.

Although the condition of the bullets fired into Mary Beth Sowers made a ballistics match with the bullets from the bar impossible, an expert was able to show a match of the ejection and firing pin marks on the .25 caliber shell casings found by Sowers's body with the ones found near Miller, indicating that the couple was shot with the same weapon.

Also counted on for the State's case was the testimony of the fraternity brother who witnessed the abduction and took down the license plate number of the abductee's Oldsmobile. It was registered to Charlene Adell Williams, who turned out to be Charlene Adell Gallego, wife of Gerald Gallego.

Add in other circumstantial and physical evidence, and the D.A. appeared to have enough to convict Gerald and Charlene Gallego for the kidnapping-execution of Mary Beth Sowers and Craig Miller.

Then a strange new twist came about. Charlene Gallego dropped a bombshell on her new attorneys when she confessed that Miller and Sowers had been but the last of a string of abductions and murders that spanned twenty-six months and stretched across three states. Ten people were dead, she said, all but one females.

According to Charlene, she had acted as the lure and her husband, Gerald, had sexually assaulted and brutalized most of the victims before killing them. It was all part of a "sex slave fantasy" Gerald had created. Only it turned into a deadly reality for ten innocent victims, plus an unborn child who never got the opportunity to know the meaning of the word innocent.

Suddenly Charlene had gained the attention of investigators from three states. A number of unsolved crimes—at least two of which had not technically even been considered criminal offenses—were soon to be connected to Gerald and Charlene Gallego.

Charlene's attorneys hired a private investigator to "check out her story." Slowly but surely it became obvious that it was all too true.

The first victims had been Kippi Vaught and Rhonda Scheffler, ages sixteen and seventeen, respectively. The police had seemed determined to pin their murders on two young black men who were identified as being with the girls in a Pontiac Firebird the day they were abducted. It turned out the detectives had been on the wrong trail the whole time.

The last victims were Craig Miller and Mary Beth Sowers, college sweethearts who never made it to that planned New Year's Eve day wedding.

In between were eight others, one of whom was several months into her pregnancy.

But Charlene was not prepared to be more specific, much less help corroborate her story, until a deal could be made. In spite of her coldhearted willfulness as an accomplice to so many murders and fear of her brutal husband and co-perpetrator, this woman was no fool. She still had that high IQ to draw on at times like this. She was not about to solve the police's crimes for them without getting something significant in return.

Charlene Gallego and her attorneys had backed the prosecution into a proverbial corner. The prosecutor knew she was as guilty as hell of kidnapping and killing Mary Sowers and Craig Miller, if only in luring them to their violent deaths with her innocent deadly charm.

But why settle for two murders if they could effectively solve ten at once? The idea took on greater prominence with the Shirley Decision by the California Supreme Court, which, in effect, barred hypnotic questioning as a law enforcement weapon in the state. This meant that the fraternity brother's eyewitness testimony, including writing down the license plate number of the Oldsmobile, was ruled inadmissible in a court of law.

Although the fraternity brother's testimony was not mandatory in getting a conviction, it certainly was a serious blow to the district attorney's case against the Gallegos.

The best bet now seemed to be, albeit with much reluctance, to make a deal with Charlene Gallego before this whole thing somehow blew up in the prosecution's face.

So the protracted negotiations between attorneys began.

Charlene Gallego, who had decided to betray her husband and look out for number one, was about to literally get away with murder and much more . . .

THIRTEEN

Karen Chipman Twiggs and Stacy Ann Redican had not returned from the Sunrise Mall soon enough for Carol Twiggs, Karen's mother. She was supposed to meet with her daughter that afternoon. When the girls failed to show up on time, Carol Twiggs had an instinctive feeling that something was very wrong.

Even her motherly instincts could not have prepared Carol Twiggs for what had happened to her daughter and friend.

Twiggs went to the mall in search of the pair, but came up with nothing. That night of April 24, 1980, she went to the Sacramento Police Department to report Karen and Stacy as missing.

Once again, the issue of runaways, as was common for such "disappearances," was brought up.

Carol Twiggs was forced to admit that Stacy Redican had a history of running away and, in fact, had run away from home when she came to live with Karen and her, a single mother. However, noted Carol Twiggs, Karen had never run away and was not unhappy as far as she knew.

Even if the police had gone along with a mother's staunch defense of her daughter, their natural inclination was to believe Stacy had run away again and persuaded Karen to jump ship with her.

Nevertheless, the search was on for the missing teenagers. They had been classmates at a Reno high school and had become close friends. Karen and her mother moved to Sacramento in 1979, only to have Stacy show up a few days later looking for a place to live. It seemed like the perfect arrangement for the girls.

Bulletins were dispatched by the Sacramento Police Department in the coming days following Twiggs and Redican's disappearance in hopes of finding the girls. Photograph posters of Karen and Stacy were also circulated throughout Sacramento County.

Neither sight nor sound of the girls surfaced for months. The police may have stuck to the runaway theory, but Carol Twiggs's instincts proved she knew her daughter better than any police detective could have.

On July 27, 1980, more than three months after

Karen Chipman Twiggs and Stacy Ann Redican disappeared, picnickers discovered their coyote-ravaged remains in two shallow graves in an area about twenty miles outside of Lovelock, Nevada.

The victims had been raped and suffered massive and fatal head injuries by a "hammer or hammer-like instrument," according to the pathologist who performed the autopsy. One victim's hands were tied behind her back; the other's hands were missing altogether, undoubtedly the cruel result of decomposition or ravenous prairie wolves.

A week after the corpses had been found, Stacy Redican's mother, sensing one was her daughter, handed over Stacy's dental charts to the Washoe County Sheriff's Department. It was discovered, coincidentally, that Karen Twigg's dentist worked in the same building as Stacy Redican's dentist. Karen's dental charts could also be compared with the teeth of the murder victims.

The dead girls were positively identified as Stacy Ann Redican and Karen Chipman Twiggs. Neither would reach their eighteenth birthday.

Finding their killer or killers would not be easy. As it turned out, the task may have proven impossible had one of the assailants not admitted to the crimes as a measure of desperation several months after the fact.

*   *   *

There were no solid clues or answers as to why the teenagers were abducted, sexually assaulted, and taken out into the Nevada desert and brutally murdered.

This did not stop the local authorities from trying to find the parties responsible for this tragedy. Sheriff James Kay McIntosh and District Attorney Richard Wagner of Pershing County, Nevada would have liked nothing better than to have Gerald and Charlene Gallego in custody and put on trial for the kidnapping-murders of Twiggs and Redican. The problem was the sheriff and D.A. were as yet unfamiliar with the Gallegos and still months away from even being close to connecting the husband and wife serial slayers to the local deaths. It would be nearly four years until a Nevada trial would take place and justice served.

In the meantime, Tom Moots and John Compston, investigators with the Nevada Bureau of Investigation, were recruited by McIntosh and Wagner to lend their assistance, expertise, and the Bureau's financial resources to the case. This practice was a veritable necessity in large counties where undersized law enforcement agencies were ill equipped to handle prolonged and expensive investigations.

Moots and Compston tracked down every possible lead from Nevada to the Sunrise Mall in Citrus Heights, and back again. Sacramentans and

Nevadans alike were questioned, interviewed, and dismissed as possible witnesses or perpetrators.

The search to find out who murdered Stacy Redican and Karen Twiggs was to continue into the fall, with little progress. Unfortunately, murder did not come in well-spaced stages. People were being abducted, assaulted, and killed daily. No matter how important it was to relatives and friends, law enforcement officials could only devote so much time and effort to each case.

Perhaps this was what Gerald and Charlene Gallego were counting on as they left the bodies of the seventeen-year-olds in shallow graves in Limerick Canyon, to be dismembered by coyotes, maggots, desert heat, and giving them three month's time to distance themselves from their deed.

FOURTEEN

Charlene knew that unmistakable feeling in her body. She was pregnant again. She decided she was only a few weeks into the pregnancy based on her missed period.

She was going to keep this baby, she thought determinedly. If Gerry didn't want it, he could go to hell. He probably would anyway, she realized.

It had only been days since Gerry had buried his latest sex slaves. There was nothing in the paper about the girls. A good sign, thought Charlene, relieved that they were once again in the free and clear. She wondered how much longer their luck would last?

Would twenty more girls fall prey to her and then Gerry?

Maybe one hundred sex slaves?

Could this weird and crazy sexual fantasy of his go on indefinitely?

Charlene did not care to look that far ahead. Right now she was more interested in her baby. Would it be a boy or girl? Would it look more like her or Gerry? How would she talk Gerry into letting her keep this one? . . .

Gerald did not want a child complicating his life, make no mistake about that, but he did not reject Charlene's pregnancy in his usual foul-mouthed, vociferous, insulting way.

Here was a man who had murdered six girls and was looking for more sex slaves. In the interim, he could use some stability in his life. Having a kid would keep Charlene happy and devoted, and give him the appearance of being a doting dad. What a joke! he thought. He and kids didn't work out too well—at least not in the normal way.

Hopefully it would be another girl who would grow up to look just like her mommy. Make that Krista.

On Saturday, May 31, 1980, the Gallegos and a couple of friends made plans to go rafting down the American River. Only Mother Nature's fury in the form of rain squelched their desires. Instead, the four ended up at Gerald and Charlene's apartment for an "impromptu" party and some heavy drinking.

Gerald, using his alias Stephen Feil, slurred to his male friend: "I want to marry Charlene. Let's go to Reno."

The friend, of course, had no idea they were already married—as Gerald and Charlene Gallego.

The four headed to Reno, having to stop several times because Charlene was experiencing morning sickness. Just after midnight, they arrived at the Washoe County Courthouse, then proceeded across the street to the Heart of Reno Wedding Chapel.

The blushing bride was dressed in an eye-catching green silk gown and a white shawl. The groom wore a black three-piece suit. Gerald may have looked the part, but his motives were not to make an honest woman out of Charlene for the second time. Rather, he was looking to solidify his hold on her should their already strained relationship somehow fall apart. He could not allow that to happen. Not after everything they had gone through together.

But Gerald had a second, even stronger reason for this hastily decided upon marriage. He somehow believed that marrying Charlene as Stephen Feil would cover all bases in protecting himself. This way his twice-married wife could surely never testify against him in the unlikely event they were ever arrested for the murder of those girls.

If he thought for an instant that Charlene would

ever squeal on him, he would just as soon see her dead, mused the groom as his bloodshot eyes gazed at the bride-to-be.

Shortly after midnight on June 1, 1980, Gerald and Charlene officially became Mr. and Mrs. Stephen Robert Feil. By then Charlene was six weeks pregnant and counting.

A few days later, the newlyweds had friends over for steak, salad, drinks, and cocaine. Ex-acquaintances have said that Charlene was the heavier user of cocaine, while Gerald was more heavily into drinking. Both Gallegos were regular marijuana smokers.

That weekend, the foursome planned a trip to the Oregon coast. Only some misunderstandings and physical abuse by Gerald towards the female of the other couple derailed those plans. The Gallegos made the trek alone.

Gold Beach is one of Oregon's many hidden treasures. The Rogue River runs through this rugged, breathtaking stretch along the coast between Brookings and Coos Bay. A variety of shops counted on tourists to take home a little of Gold Beach with them. Few could imagine such an idyllic place as the scene of a brutal murder.

But few could imagine the psychopathic personality of Gerald Gallego and a more than willing accomplice in his wife, twice over, Charlene.

On June 7, 1980, just days after the couple's second marriage, they reached Gold Beach, following
a drive that took them through parts of the Cas-
cades, Klamath Falls, and some small coastal
towns.

Neither Gerald nor Charlene had particularly enjoyed the trip thus far. When they were not arguing, they were lost in their own thoughts. Charlene
was wishing she was home, where she could better
tolerate the downside of pregnancy. Gerald, on the
other hand, was happy to be here in the rugged
outdoors. He only wished it was with someone
other than Charlene.

Then he saw her. A woman was walking by the
side of the road, all by her lonesome. Long hair,
bouncy strut, not so bad looking. Her belly was
sticking out. Just what he needed, Gerald frowned,
another pregnant woman.

But she would have to do.

Charlene noticed her too. Only she assumed they
would pass her by. At least she hoped so. The lady
was pregnant, she observed. Don't mess with a
pregnant woman, Gerry, she said to herself. As far
as she was concerned, that was crossing the line.

Gerald had other ideas.

"Let's give the lady a lift," he said sweetly.

"Let's not," replied Charlene firmly. "Can't you
see she's pregnant!"

"So are you," he scoffed. "You ought to know

by now, I like my women pregnant . . ."

Linda Aguilar, twenty-one, was four months pregnant with her second child. She had picked up some items from a local store and was on her way home, even though things were not going very well with her and her boyfriend.

When the van pulled alongside·her, she had paid it little attention until she heard a man's voice say: "How 'bout a ride?"

She looked and saw a young woman on the passenger side and a man in his mid-thirties behind the wheel. Linda Aguilar might have said, "No thanks" or "I'd rather walk." That just might have been enough to dissuade Gerald Gallego.

Instead, she said just what he wanted to hear: "Sure, why not?" She smiled at the nice couple, who smiled back. How safe could one be?

The van and its new passenger crossed the Rogue River bridge. Another vehicle crossed from the opposite direction. The driver, who had noticed the pregnant woman on foot earlier, had planned to offer her a ride himself. Only the van had gotten there first.

A few seconds would have made the difference in life or death for the soon-to-be victim.

Gerald was becoming more reckless in his abductions, thought Charlene. A pregnant woman with still plenty of daylight left? Why, Gerry? she wondered, frightened.

On top of that, she considered, this woman didn't even seem like his type. At least not the type he had led Charlene to believe he fantasized about: girlish-looking, blonde, slender, cute—just like her. This woman had dark hair, a dark complexion, was obviously not slim these days, and was not particularly attractive.

Why, Gerry? Charlene asked herself again.

Then, strangely, she engaged in small talk with the unsuspecting woman sitting in the back of the van. After all, they did have something in common—a child on the way.

"It's time," Gerald told his wife in no uncertain terms.

She may have argued the point, if only for the sake of the baby the woman was carrying. But by now Charlene had decided, what's the use?

"Take the wheel," he said.

She did, while Gerald climbed into the back. He surprised his prey by sticking his .357 in her face. The niceties were over.

Charlene knew the routine by now. He would bind the woman's hands, establish her complete obedience through fear and intimidation, and brutally rape her, along with any other forced sex acts that suited his fancy. And that was only for starters.

She wondered how Gerry would rate his pregnant slave. Could she possibly satisfy him?

Frankly, thought Charlene, sex was the last thing she wanted from Gerry while she was pregnant. Especially when she was sick, which seemed to be all the time.

But then, she did not believe for an instant that his latest slave actually wanted what he was forcing upon her. Who in their right mind, pregnant or not, would?

Gerald resumed driving and before long parked in a grassy area where there seemed to be little chance of him being interrupted. Charlene got out of the van.

"Hey, where you goin'?" asked Gerald, more curious than concerned.

She sneered. "Where can I go, really . . . ?"

He smiled. Nowhere, bitch. Not if you know what's good for you.

Charlene padded through the grass and around the van haphazardly. The last thing she wanted to see or hear was him screwing a pregnant woman. It was disgusting.

Maybe that's why Gerry was doing this, it occurred to Charlene. To punish me for getting pregnant. He would take out his frustrations against me on this poor woman.

When Gerald was through inside, he exited the van. Drenched in sweat, he looked as if he had been given a real workout, Charlene observed. What condition must his sex slave be in?

"I gave it one helluva try," Gerald huffed. "Pregnant women can be a bitch when it comes to putting out." He grinned lewdly. "I guess you'd know something about that, wouldn't you?"

Charlene frowned at him. "The father of that baby is probably looking for her."

The smile left his face. "Let him look," he said confidently. "I doubt he'll ever find her."

They got back into the van. If Charlene had thought it was possible that Gerald might let this one live, he had just erased all doubts. Any living sex slaves could come back to haunt him. And he didn't believe in ghosts.

Charlene emotionlessly handed the naked sex slave her clothing while glancing at her protruding belly. Like Gerry, she looked as if she had been put through the ringer—only much worse. It was a wonder she could even still function after what Charlene imagined Gerry had put her through. She watched as Linda Aguilar, her breathing erratic, face flushed and damp from tears, hypnotically and sloppily dressed.

Gerald drove, shouting expletives as he took to the road. The pregnant bitch hadn't done a damned thing to get him up, he cursed. All she did was whine like the bastard she was carrying. He would soon put both out of their misery.

Charlene sat beside her husband like the zombie she had become when his sexual urges took control of him—and her. Occasionally she glanced back at the latest object of Gerry's desires and fantasies. The woman's hands were bound behind her back and she was whimpering and sniffing. Charlene wondered if the nylon rope was cutting off her circulation.

Or maybe it was the child she carried that was really bothering her. Charlene knew something about that. Even now, she felt like she was going to throw up.

Gerald found the place he was looking for. Sand, trees, isolation. The ideal getaway for his pregnant sex slave. He grabbed his .357 and forced her out of the van. Like the others, he gave her a fake song and dance about no harm coming to her. As if he had not already inflicted major damage.

Charlene watched from outside the van as Gerry led his captive past a rock formation and out of her view. She expected to hear pops from his .357 Magnum at any time. It never happened. She felt a false sense of relief. She hated the thought of shooting someone and leaving them for dead.

Darkness had rolled in and Charlene stared at the half moon, her thoughts elsewhere, anywhere but here. That was one way she coped with this. Try not to think about it, she told herself. She had found moderate success with this approach.

Gerald's absence was less than half an hour. As always, he returned alone.

He bragged to Charlene about beating his pregnant slave with a rock, then strangling her for good measure. It was almost as if he expected her to applaud his brutality and cold-bloodedness.

Instead, she sneered and asked: "What do we do with her bag?" She had looked inside and saw that it contained toys. Were they for her unborn child? Or did she have other children who would now be forever deprived of their mother?

"We'll bury it," Gerald said.

Then he decided they had better not waste any more time hanging around the beach. Someone might see them.

They took the bag with them and Charlene tossed it in a garbage can a few miles up the road.

Another victim was dead and, it appeared to Charlene, as usual, no one would ever know they had anything to do with it.

FIFTEEN

Two days after Linda Aguilar's abduction, her live-in boyfriend, Rick, reported her missing to the Sheriff's Department in Port Orford, Oregon. The twenty-three-year-old drywaller said that Linda was twenty-one, about four months pregnant, and the mother of his two-year-old son.

He also noted that Linda was prone to wandering off on her own, sometimes for days at a time, as a nature buff. Interestingly enough, after "only" two days of "wandering," Rick found it necessary to report her missing.

The Curry County Sheriff's Department made some inquiries, but likely had no reason to suspect foul play. Witnesses in nearby Wedderburn and Gold Beach reported seeing the pregnant Linda on foot, in stores, and at a tavern, but not apparently in imminent danger. Friends said that she had openly spoken of needing time alone.

Linda appeared to have left home of her own accord and for her own purposes, became the official conclusion. At twenty-one, she was not subject to curfew or her boyfriend's concerns, mild as they were.

But when Linda Aguilar failed to surface after a week or so, investigators did an about-face and decided that she may have been the victim of a crime. The drywaller boyfriend, who did not seem overly distraught about her absence, became the obvious prime suspect in her disappearance.

More questioning of friends and acquaintances gave further rise to the possibility that Rick may have had something to do with Linda's unknown whereabouts. By most accounts, the couple's relationship had been stormy at best and downright violent at worst. Rick was known to have a short fuse and was not afraid to use Linda as a punching bag.

Things were not looking good for the drywaller, who denied any wrongdoing. Certainly not murder.

At least two people could vouch for him, had they been willing to come forward.

On the evening of June 22, 1980, German tourists, probably hoping to discover some hidden treasures on the Oregon Coast, instead found the remains of Linda Aguilar. Actually, it was the couple's dog that first was attracted to the strong stench in an area behind some rocks.

When the Germans caught up with their ferociously barking dog, they saw why. Beneath the sand was the horrifying sight of a badly decomposed body. The couple quickly notified authorities.

Few people doubted that "Jane Doe" was actually Linda Aguilar—what was left of her. The pieces of identification found with the body all confirmed this, more or less.

The autopsy gave a chilling account of the excruciating ordeal Linda Aguilar had been put through before she died. Her hands and feet bound, she had been bludgeoned repeatedly on the head, cracking her skull. This probably would have killed her, if not for her strong will to live.

Sand was discovered in the decedent's mouth, throat and lungs. This led the medical examiner to conclude that the blows to the head had only temporarily stunned her. It was at this time that her assailant buried her in the sand at Gold Beach. When she awakened, Linda was unable to free herself from her binds or the sand around her, though she had frantically tried. She suffocated in her sandy grave.

The terrible truth was in. Linda Aguilar, carrying a four-month-old baby, had been buried alive.

With Linda Aguilar's fate no longer in doubt, the fingers pointed more and more at her boyfriend, Rick.

In fact, he had already left town for the friendlier confines of California, prior to the discovery of Linda's body. A natural reaction for an innocent person facing growing hostilities from a community he and Linda had called home.

Rick returned to Oregon voluntarily and appeared more than willing to cooperate with the Curry County Sheriff's Department. After all, he had nothing to hide. Trouble was, everything that was out in the open seemed to further incriminate him.

Friends of the couple provided police with more accounts of girlfriend battering and alleged group sex in which he and Linda had participated. Police also found bloodstains in the bedroom of their trailer. These became apparent when officers, armed with a search warrant, sprayed luminal, a material that glows in the dark when in contact with bloodstains otherwise invisible to the human eye.

Even a lie detector test went against the young drywaller, and it seemed only a matter of time before he was charged with Linda Aguilar's murder.

Another possibility that had been given less attention was the report by a passerby of a pregnant woman entering a yellow van in Gold Beach. The witness, who had expressed interest in giving the woman a ride had the van's occupants not stopped to pick her up, identified that woman as Linda Aguilar.

Under hypnosis, the witness tried to provide more details to detectives. He described a muscular man behind the wheel of the van and possibly a small woman beside him.

This might have put the law on the trail of the real killers of Linda Aguilar, had the witnesses description of the van been accurate. A license plate number tucked away in the subconscious mind would also have done the trick.

Instead, police began a search for a yellow rather than off-white van with mountains and vultures painted on the sides. Not too surprisingly, the search turned up nothing and no one.

Once more, Gerald and Charlene Gallego had evaded the authorities for the time being, as circumstances and lady luck continued to work in their favor.

SIXTEEN

Charlene Gallego had found a way to spare her own life and ultimately become a free woman while young enough to be able to make something of it. The price was to testify against Gerald Gallego, her husband and the father of her nearly two-year-old son, Gerald, Jr. Her testimony was almost sure to get Gallego the death penalty, if convicted.

It was a price Charlene was prepared to pay.

On November 10, 1982, after months of negotiations with the district attorneys of California, Nevada, and Oregon, Charlene Adell Gallego pled guilty to two counts of first-degree murder in the deaths of Craig Miller and Mary Elizabeth Sowers.

In exchange for her testimony against her husband, Charlene was given a "guaranteed" sentence of sixteen years, eight months—a sentence equal to the minimum time that must be served in California for a first-degree murder, given a twenty-five years to life sentence. The sentence was to be served in its entirety, without possibility of parole, but was subject to approval by the California Board of Prison Terms. Charlene was credited with the two years she had already served.

The bulk of Charlene's prison term was actually to take place in Nevada where, under a similar plea bargain agreement, she pled guilty to the second-degree murders of Stacy Redican and Karen Twiggs. Her sentence was the same determinate length of sixteen years, eight months. In return, Charlene was to testify against Gallego, for the kidnap-murders of four girls in Nevada, including Redican and Twiggs.

No one seemed happy about the relatively light sentence given the confessed murderess of a minimum of four people, least of all the family and friends of the victims. Charlene, who had implicated her husband in the sex-motivated murder of ten people, had been granted immunity from prosecution for essentially all but two second-degree murders.

Prosecutor Jim Morris sought to put the best spin on a bad situation. "By [Charlene] disclosing her involvement in several additional murders, she has created a compelling argument that she deserves no leniency for herself," he said. "The focus, however, cannot just be limited to her alone. All ten victims and both defendants must be considered together for the purposes of obtaining at least substantial justice."

Morris went on to say: "It is rare that total justice is ever obtained in a case of this magnitude, especially when considering the pitfalls of a trial, the rulings on a myriad of motions, the uncertainties attending an appeal, and the final issue of whether a death sentence, life without parole, or natural life mean, in fact, what they say, especially as demonstrated in California."

The State of Oregon's role in the negotiations was limited to a signature. Although it now had two solid suspects to replace one in the murder of the four months pregnant Linda Aguilar, Oregon elected to defer the cost of prosecuting her killer to the death penalty states of California and Nevada.

From Charlene Gallego's standpoint, she had avoided the worst of the justice system and placed virtually the entire burden of the crimes she had co-perpetrated on her husband.

Even then, she would face challenges to her sweet deal from California and Nevada authorities who found it a bit too sweet for their liking.

In December of 1982, the Washoe County District Attorney refused to ratify the negotiated plea bargain agreement. It was not until February 25, 1983 that his successor, Mills Lane, signed the agreement and grant of immunity, making it official in Nevada.

Charlene had been perfectly willing to plead guilty to first-degree murder in the deaths of Karen Twiggs and Stacy Redican rather than second-degree had the plea bargain terms remained the same. However, Nevada law prevented the short length of sixteen years, eight months sentence for first-degree murder. Second-degree charges were more appropriate for the agreement, if not the crime.

Having survived this scare, Charlene's California plea bargain appeared in jeopardy in November of 1983, when the State Board of Prison Terms refused to ratify the terms of the agreement. At issue was the sixteen year, eight month prison term negotiated between prosecutors from three states.

Chairman of the Board Rudolph Castro rejected the agreement on the grounds that "it was important we would not usurp our responsibilities on the basis of a plea bargain." He also noted that the board was not a party to any of the negotiations that led to the plea bargain.

A possible battle within the California justice system never emerged as a Sacramento County Superior Court judge dropped the first-degree murder charges Charlene had pled guilty to in the deaths of Mary Beth Sowers and Craig Miller.

Charlene, who was present as the judge read the

thirteen-page decision, smiled upon hearing it. And with good reason. The judge's ruling meant that Charlene—who had lured Miller and Sowers to their deaths—was henceforth free and clear of any California charges to that effect. She now only had to serve her time in Nevada and walk away without looking back.

With the plea bargain in place, Charlene Gallego opened up to investigators, providing victims' names, dates, places, details that only the killers could have known. The roll call was eerily distressing for the families of the victims:

Rhonda Martin Scheffler
Kippi Vaught
Brenda Lynne Judd
Sandra Kay Colley
Karen Chipman Twiggs
Stacy Ann Redican
Linda Aguilar
Virginia Mochel
Craig Miller
Mary Beth Sowers

And an unborn child who was halfway there until its life was snuffed out.

Charlene led the brigade of investigators from one site of her and Gerald Gallego's sex-motivated murderous odyssey to another. The trek crossed three states. From Baxter, high up in the Sierras of

California; to Gold Beach on Oregon's rugged coast; to rural Placer County in California; investigators were able to trace the path of possibly the country's first serial slaying couple.

Charlene's remarkable gift for detail and accuracy made the job of gathering evidence that much easier for law enforcement investigators and technicians. Nevertheless, evidence was hardly in abundance. In some cases it was nonexistent. Time, seasonal changes, shifts in the earth, decomposition of bodies, destroyed or disposed of evidence, all contributed to limiting what could be found and used against Gerald Gallego.

The strongest California case was for the kidnapping-murder of coeds Craig Miller and Mary Beth Sowers. Although the prosecution was without the testimony of Miller's fraternity brother who had witnessed the abduction and handed police the vital license plate number of what proved to be the getaway car of the killers, there was enough other ammunition to make for a strong case against Gallego.

Most prominent was the ballistics match of the .25 caliber bullets that entered and killed Craig Miller and bullets fired into the ceiling of a tavern by bartender Gerald Gallego. Although the gun used was never found, circumstantial evidence pointed towards a .25 caliber Beretta automatic, which gun registration records indicated had been purchased by Charlene Gallego in March of 1980.

The Beretta was consistent with the weapon used to kill Miller and Sowers, which had a barrel with a right-hand twist.

A match of the ejection and firing pin marks on the shell casings found near both Miller and Sowers's bodies further supported the contention that both were shot with the same gun.

Then, of course, there was Charlene Gallego's eyewitness account of the kidnapping and murder of Miller and Sowers to nail the lid on her husband's coffin.

The prosecution, partly through Charlene's cooperation, was also able to build a solid supportive case against Gallego in the murders of Kippi Vaught and Rhonda Martin Scheffler, the first two of his ten alleged sex-motivated slayings.

Gallego's semen and blood types were shown to match specimens taken from the undergarments of Rhonda Scheffler's corpse. This was not the case for Scheffler's husband or the black suspects in her murder. In each instance, blood tests came back negative.

Fibers found on Scheffler and Vaught's clothing proved to be a match with carpet fibers taken from the van the Gallegos had used to kidnap the pair.

Another strong piece of evidence linking Gallego to Vaught and Scheffler came in the form of "bracken fern." The material was found amongst vegetation in the victims' socks and shoes. Experts found the fern to be consistent with that present in the Baxter area, where Charlene Gallego claimed her husband had sexually assaulted the two girls. In the Sloughhouse area, where Vaught and Scheffler's bodies were discovered, no such bracken fern was in existence.

The weapon believed to have killed Kippi Vaught and Rhonda Scheffler was an FIE (Firearms Import-Export) .25 caliber automatic revolver that Charlene had purchased in December 1977, from a Del Paso Heights sporting goods store. Once again, the weapon itself had long since been disposed of. However, its particulars were consistent with the weapon that killed Scheffler and Vaught, which had six lands and grooves along with a left-hand twist.

The deck was becoming stacked against Gerald Gallego as a trial date approached.

In November 1982, a "fully cooperating" Charlene Gallego accompanied investigators to her parents' home in search of evidence the D.A.'s office hoped to use against Gerald Gallego.

The trip proved to be fruitful, if for another trial. Physical evidence was seized that would later be significant in Nevada's prosecution of Gallego.

As a reward for her cooperation, Charlene was

given the opportunity to see her one-year-old son, Gerald Gallego, Jr., and her still supportive parents, Charles and Mercedes Williams.

In the meantime, the trial had been moved to Martinez in Contra Costa County, some thirty miles from San Francisco. The change of venue was almost a given with the local publicity the case had generated and the unlikelihood of finding twelve unbiased witnesses in Sacramento County.

Gerald Gallego, who must have been infuriated that his two times around wife—and girl without heart—had sold him down the river by cooperating with the prosecution, decided that the best chance he had to win this case was to represent himself. So he sent his public defender walking and now faced the greatest challenge of his thirty-five plus years. He would have to go head to head against his back-stabbing wife and convince a jury of his peers that he was a wrongfully accused man on all counts. At stake, he knew by now, was not just his freedom but almost certainly his life, if found guilty of the multiple murder charges.

The State of Nevada was anxiously awaiting the beginning and end of Gallego's California trial, for it had second at bat and was getting antsy. The District Attorney of Pershing County, Richard Wagner, planned to prosecute Gerald Gallego for the brutal kidnapping, assault, and murders of

Karen Chipman Twiggs, Stacy Redican, Brenda Judd, and Sandra Colley, regardless of the outcome of the Martinez trial. It was the very least Nevada could do for the victims who died such senseless, horrible deaths in the desert state.

And Nevada, unlike California, had no qualms about putting multiple murderers to death.

Unfortunately, Wagner and company would have to wait their turn. California had the first crack at Gerald Gallego and it fully intended to make it count.

SEVENTEEN

In spite of the murderous tryst that bound Gerald and Charlene together, the couple was struggling to stay together during the summer of 1980. Both were heavily abusing drugs and alcohol, perhaps each in their own way trying to cope with the secrets they carried.

Gerald was becoming bolder and bolder in his sex fantasy conquests and Charlene had to feel that this recklessness would catch up with them sooner or later—probably sooner. If it was up to her, they would just quit while they were ahead. But she knew that Gerry, stubborn and macho as ever, would never give up his sex slave desires. Not until he was caught, and maybe killed.

And what about her? Would she end up in prison some day? Or would Gerry do to her what he had done to seven other women?

It was her fear of both answers that likely kept Charlene from blowing the whistle on her husband even as the killings mounted.

Their personal troubles continued as Gerald was fired from his job at the Bob-Les Club in early July. As usual, the Gallegos drowned their sorrows in alcohol, mostly beer and vodka, and drugs; marijuana and cocaine. Neither seemed particularly concerned about protecting the health of the baby that Charlene was carrying.

One legal pastime the couple engaged in was fishing. It was more to Gerald's liking than Charlene's, but this was often the case in everything the two did together.

On the night of July 16, 1980, Gerald and Charlene spent a few hours at the Sacramento River hoping to catch something worthwhile. Unfortunately, few fish went for the bait. In between long waits, the Gallegos drank themselves silly. Charlene kept pace with Gerald in drinks, and paid the price. Alcohol and pregnancy did not mix very well, inducing nausea and vomiting.

By the time they abandoned their unsuccessful fishing trip, the couple ended up in West Sacramento, where working class residents lived in tiny homes and trailer parks and cheap motels were frequented by streetwalkers and their johns.

The Gallegos came upon the Sail Inn, a local tav-

ern, and decided that more drinking was in order.
Inside, they made themselves at home, chatting
amicably with other patrons, drinking, and playing
pool.

The bartender, Virginia Mochel, had a reputation
of being sociable with the customers but certainly
not sleazy or looking for trouble. The same could
be said of Charlene as she glanced only in passing
at the slender blonde-haired woman in her mid-
thirties. Trouble was the last thing Charlene
wanted or needed as the alcohol played tricks on
her mind and body. All she wanted was to go
home, sleep it off, and deal with tomorrow when
it came.

Convincing her husband, however, would not be
easy. Gerry was playing pool and talking boister-
ously. She heard him tell the men around the table
that his name was Stephen and that he worked as
a bartender at the Argonaut Club in Del Paso
Heights.

This was news to her. As far as she knew he was
still looking for work—and not very seriously at
that.

They stayed at the tavern until closing time.
Charlene had noted Gerry eyeing the pretty bartender, but thought little of it. He was always going
to look, she knew. Surely he would not even consider trying to add her to his list of sex kittens?

The Gallegos stumbled to the van, where Gerald

151

informed Charlene that he was not quite ready to leave. Charlene detected that all too familiar lilt in his voice.

"Don't be stupid, Gerry!" she begged.

He glared at her with drunken eyes. "Hey, who the hell are you calling stupid, bitch!"

"Let's just go home, please." She gave him a tired sigh.

"I'll decide when we go," he growled.

When he finally started the van, Charlene thought she had talked some sense into him. As usual, she was wrong.

Gerald stopped the van near the car the lady bartender had just gotten into. Before Charlene could utter another word of protest, Gerry had grabbed his .357 Magnum and left her sitting alone in the van.

It was one-thirty in the morning when Virginia Mochel, thirty-four, advised the Sail Inn patrons that the bar was closing. At the time, there were two regulars, three young men from the nearby rice mill; and the couple, Stephen and Charlene, in the bar.

By two o'clock everyone had gone and Virginia was soon to follow suit. She was anxious to get home and tuck in her two children, Petra, nine, and Wesley, four. She phoned the alarm company to tell them she was setting the alarm for the night. A routine pain in the ass, but better safe than sorry.

Just after two on the morning of July 17, 1980, Virginia Mochel locked up the tavern and headed for her car. She had barely gotten inside when she heard the knock on the window and saw the familiar face of the man named Stephen from the bar. She rolled down the window.

Only then did she see the .357 Magnum revolver pointed at her face.

Gerald Gallego was celebrating his thirty-fourth birthday as he forced the bartender at gunpoint into the back of the van. Once again he had a sex slave to do his bidding. So she didn't look as much like Charlene as the others—not counting the pregnant whore. This was his birthday and she, like it or not, was going to be his present.

Charlene didn't like this at all. Why her? She was older, not Gerry's type. Why the hell was he taking such dangerous risks? Charlene wondered. The parking lot was well lit. Anyone could have seen him take the lady bartender. Maybe what he really wanted, she considered, was to be caught . . . ?

The sex slave was tied up in the back, Gerry drove, and Charlene sat by his side—sick from too much alcohol and the thought of what he was going to do to this one.

Virginia Mochel talked about her two young children, the baby-sitter, bartending—anything to appeal to her captors to get out of this with no more harm than had already been done in her being kidnapped.

Gerald responded in his normal friendly way just before he was to zoom in for the kill. Charlene wondered where they were headed on I-80 East. Baxter again? Reno? Lovelock?

"We're going home," Gerald informed her calmly.

"Don't do this to me, Gerry," she urged fiercely. "Not in our home!"

He grinned. "If that's the way you feel," he slurred, "the van will do just fine."

Virginia, sensing what was to come, opted for death over violation and degradation, and requested such. Her captors would not hear of it—at least not yet.

Gerald parked at the apartment on Woodhollow Way and Charlene went inside. She felt sick to her stomach and made it to the bathroom in time to vomit. This made her feel a little better.

There was no way for her to get rid of the anger—maybe hatred—she was starting to feel for Gerry for what he was putting her through. These urges he had were getting to be tiresome and dangerous. He didn't know when to leave well enough alone.

Charlene waited impatiently as Gerry did his thing in the van with the bartender. She tried watching television, but there was nothing on at that hour. There were inaudible sounds coming from the van that Charlene imagined the whole world could probably hear.

Finally Gerry came in after Charlene had nearly fallen asleep on the couch.

"I'm finished!" he shouted at her.

"Do you want me to congratulate you?" Charlene said with sarcasm. She had always had a quick tongue, even against Gerry. Being intoxicated made it that much quicker.

"No," he muttered. "Just get the hell up and c'mon."

She obeyed as she had been trained to do.

"Why don't you kill me, you bastard?" sputtered Virginia Mochel from the bed in the back of the van where she had been violently sexually assaulted. Her worst fears had come true, along with the emptiness for living after such an ordeal.

Virginia repeated her desire to be killed while Gerald drove and Charlene sat in the passenger seat, confused. Had what he done to the lady bartender been so horrendous that she would rather be dead than alive? wondered Charlene. What the hell had he done to her?

Charlene suddenly felt a lump in her throat. The bartender had been nice to them at the bar. She had two kids. She wasn't like the others. Why would Gerry pick her to be his sex slave? The lady bartender deserved a better fate, decided Charlene.

Gerry had Charlene get behind the wheel. He ordered her to turn the music up loud and not to turn around, much like when he had murdered those first two girls. Only then it was outside the van.

Was he actually going to shoot the bartender in the van?

Charlene braced herself for the shots that never came. By the time Gerald climbed back up front, she suspected what he confirmed: he had killed her with his bare hands, a new deadly weapon in his arsenal.

The lady bartender had gotten her wish.

"We've gotta get rid of her," Gerald said rapidly, not one to leave the remains of his sex slavery to be easily discovered.

They drove to an area near a levee road outside Clarksburg and Gerald proceeded to get rid of another victim. Charlene made herself peek at the bartender being dragged from the van. She was nude and her hands were bound behind her back. What had once been a pretty face was now a colorless, faceless shell. Her neck was swollen so that it no longer resembled a neck and was discolored in a kaleidoscope of dark and dreary shades.

Charlene quivered as she turned her head away. Death was horrible, she thought. At least the lady bartender was dead, she rationalized. She didn't have to see what she looked like afterwards.

Gerald, having disposed of the body, returned to

the van and they drove back to their apartment—each lost in their private thoughts.

Wee hours of the morning it was, but it was never too early as far as Gerald was concerned to give the van a thorough cleaning and get rid of any and all incriminating evidence that could tie them to the bartender. She wouldn't be history until they had.

Charlene, still suffering the effects of morning sickness and a hangover, did as the master told her. The van was her job and she did it almost flawlessly.

At least every time up until now. What Gerry didn't know probably wouldn't hurt either of them. She had to get some sleep and hope that the nightmares that usually followed his sex slave murders did not haunt her this time around.

Gerald awoke after only a few hours of sleep. He made Charlene get up.

"Rise and shine, sleepyhead," he smiled down at her. "You know what today is, don't you—my thirty-fourth birthday. Let's not waste one minute of it!"

EIGHTEEN

When Virginia Mochel failed to return home overnight, the baby-sitter reported it to the Yolo County Sheriff's Department the morning of July 17, 1980. It was highly unusual for Virginia not to so much as call had she chosen to spend the night with a man, perhaps a bar patron. She cared too much for her children to have either them or the baby-sitter worried.

Moreover, Virginia had a firm rule against mixing romance with drinks. She took her job seriously and made it clear to Sail Inn patrons that there was a certain line in her friendly disposition that she would not cross.

Friends of Virginia, noticing her car still in the tavern's parking lot that morning, became alarmed that she may have been the victim of foul play. The fact that her driver's side window was rolled down—something she allegedly never did until the car was moving—led many to believe her assailant or abductor was someone she recognized and felt safe talking to.

It did not take long for search parties to be organized. They combed the barren area bordering South River Park, which was near the Sail Inn. The search was expanded to the banks of the Sacramento River Delta, the waters around the river levees, and the Port of Sacramento area. Some loyal friends even stood in the back of a pickup truck to get an elevated view inside the thick brush as the truck rumbled along the back roads of southeastern Yolo County.

Always the search seemed to stop just short of Clarksburg. No body was found and, to most who knew her, Virginia Mochel had inexplicably disappeared without a trace, likely to never resurface alive.

In the meantime, Yolo County investigators were doing their part to try and discover what happened to the missing bartender. In interviewing regular patrons of the Sail Inn, two "strangers" that came up were a man named "Stephen" and his companion who had given the name of Charlene.

They had been drinking at the tavern late on the night of July 16th, investigators were told, and arrived there in an early 1970s Dodge recreational van. The only other clue, aside from physical descriptions of the couple, investigators had to go on was that the man named Stephen had bragged about being a bartender at the Argonaut Club in Del Paso Heights.

In fact, Gerald Gallego aka Stephen Feil actually started working for the club as a bartender on July 21st.

Two days later, Yolo County Sheriff's Detective David Trujillo—having discovered from the Argonaut Club that they had a new employee named Stephen Robert Feil and that he had a girlfriend named Charlene—telephoned Stephen Feil at work and inquired as to if he knew anything about the disappearance of Sail Inn bartender Virginia Mochel.

Stephen Feil freely admitted being at the tavern the night Virginia vanished, but said neither he nor his live-in girlfriend, Charlene, knew what had happened to the woman bartender.

"Wish I could help you," Feil said believably, "but the truth is, my girlfriend and I did some heavy drinking that night. We barely made it out without falling flat on our faces. To be honest with you, detective, there isn't a helluva lot I can remember after midnight."

Trujillo had no real reason at that point to suspect Stephen Feil or his girlfriend of any wrongdoing. Nevertheless, he followed up on the interview by phoning the girlfriend, Charlene, the next day at the couple's Woodhollow Way apartment. She gave her name as Charlene Gallego and more or less matched Stephen Feil's account of their visit to the Sail Inn on the night of July 16th.

Charlene did provide one additional piece of information that would prove to be significant months later. She told the detective that prior to arriving at the tavern, she and Stephen had spent the evening fishing in southeastern Yolo County.

At the time, however, this meant nothing in particular to Detective Trujillo. After all, fishing and drinking came with the territory in this working-class community. Besides that, there were others, such as the three men from the rice mill, who were at the Sail Inn that night who seemed to be more likely suspects in Virginia Mochel's disappearance than Stephen Feil and Charlene Gallego.

The unsolved mystery of Virginia Mochel's disappearance came to a frightening end on October 3, 1980. Fishermen discovered her nude, decomposed remains in thick brush near Clarksburg in southeastern Yolo County. The bartender and mother of two might have been found months earlier had search parties not established an "informal boundary" just before the point of discovery. Virginia's hands were bound behind her back with fishing line. The terrible condition of the corpse made it impossible to determine the cause of death or if the victim had been sexually molested. Under the circumstances, it was probably best that only her killers knew the unspeakable horrors that had been inflicted upon Virginia Mochel before her death.

Detective Trujillo, now with a body to confirm that the bartender had been murdered, went through the case file looking for any retrospective clues as to her assailant. He found a possible clue. Charlene Gallego had stated that she and her boyfriend, Stephen Feil, had gone fishing that evening. Was the fact that Virginia's hands were tied with *fishing line* coincidence?

Trujillo followed up on his hunch about as far as he could at the time. He located Charlene Gallego, who had since moved back in with her parents. Charlene's story of the night in question remained the same.

"I'm really sorry, Detective Trujillo," cooed her sweet voice, "to hear about the lady bartender. She was nice to me and Stephen when we were at the bar. I hope you find whoever did this to her!"

Trujillo might have still had his doubts about Charlene Gallego and Stephen Feil, but decided he had little choice in the absence of solid evidence than to look elsewhere for suspects in Virginia Mochel's murder.

* * *

That all changed a month later after Sacramento and El Dorado County authorities revealed that they were seeking Gerald Gallego alias Stephen Robert Feil and his wife, Charlene, in connection with the kidnapping of Craig Miller and Mary Beth Sowers and the murder of Miller. Detective Trujillo then knew instinctively that Virginia Mochel could be added to the list of people the Gallegos had abducted and killed.

That made it nine victims in all, including a twenty-one-year-old Oregon woman and her four-month-old fetus—with two more yet to come.

Trujillo soon located the recreational van the fugitive couple had driven to the Sail Inn the night of July 16, 1980, when Virginia Mochel disappeared. The Gallegos had sold the van, but left behind bloody evidence that would link them to at least two of their victims.

NINETEEN

Gerald and Charlene Gallego had narrowly avoided apprehension in the abduction and murder of Virginia Mochel. If only the police had known about the fishing line that bound Virginia's hands months *before* her body was found. Perhaps then Charlene's innocuous admission that she and Gerald had been fishing that night might have enabled authorities to put two and two together—resulting in the arrest of the murderous pair before they could kill again.

And they would kill again before their eventual capture.

Charlene was satisfied after talking with Detective Trujillo in late July 1980, that she had backed up Gerry's story about that night in convincing fashion. The detective had been friendly but suspicious. Charlene had prepared herself for the worst. Surely the detective would see right through her? Wasn't it his job to know when someone was lying to him?

Apparently he never suspected a thing, she thought. She had saved their necks that Gerry seemed determined to put on the chopping block. How could he be so stupid and careless? Charlene asked herself angrily. What was in his mind to possess him to nab that lady bartender when there were hundreds of girls out there he could have made his sex slaves with far less risk?

Charlene had to be feeling that their unusually good luck was starting to run out. Gerald was becoming more and more unstable, unpredictable, impetuous—all ingredients that were bound to blow up in his face, and hers, sooner than later.

But what was she to do about it? They had already murdered eight women. One that was, like Charlene, with child. Regardless of Charlene's anger with Gerry, there was no room for second thoughts or turning back the clock. Whatever happened, Charlene knew, she was in far too deep to abandon ship.

And Gerald knew that. He had married her twice as an insurance policy. Had he believed she would circumvent that one day to turn State's evidence against him, he would not have hesitated to add her to his long list of murder victims.

Even Gerald admitted to himself—if not to his wife—that it was a foolish thing he had done in kidnapping that bartender broad. He blamed it on being drunk and horny; even if neither truly applied. He did not really know what the hell ruled his sex fantasy slave urges. For all he knew, the devil—his dear old dad—was in him and, therefore, his destiny was signed and sealed from the day he was born.

Gerald decided that the van had become too hot. He had to get rid of it before the cops ended up somehow connecting it to the bartender, not to mention one of the slaves that got to ride in the back before her.

Sometime during the summer of 1980, the Gallegos sold the van to a couple in Orangevale who were unsuspecting of its brutal history for eight women.

The increasing strain and tension in the Gallegos' relationship continued throughout the summer. As with his five previous wives, Gerald often took out his frustrations on Charlene. Beating up on women who were physically not equipped to hurt him seemed to be one of Gerald's greatest power trips and misplaced demonstrations of machismo.

In early August 1980, Gerald lost his cool with Charlene in the presence of her mother, Mercedes Williams, who was visiting the couple at their

167

Woodhollow Way apartment. After a prolonged argument, Gerald had Charlene by the throat and was choking her.

Mercedes, hearing her daughter gasping for breath, came to her rescue. She could not believe Gerald was attacking Charlene like that. When he would not stop, Mercedes grabbed the first object she could find; which happened to be one of Gerald's many guns that was lying on the table.

She did not want to shoot him, the husband of her precious daughter. Instead, Mercedes used the barrel of the gun to pistol whip Gerald repeatedly on the side of the head. One blow only would not stop this bull of a man with hatred in his eyes.

Gerald finally released his grip on Charlene's neck and backed off. Mercedes Williams's defense of her daughter had done the trick. She had opened up a hole on the side of Gerald's head from which blood now flowed freely down his face.

The sight of this brought out the motherly instincts in Charlene. She all but forgot the ordeal she had just been put through, and went to her husband's aid.

Nevertheless, things between the Gallegos only got worse. In September 1980, Charlene did what she probably should have done the first time Gerry laid a hand on her back in 1977; or at least when he brought to her attention his sex slave fantasies the following year—she packed her belongings and moved back in with her parents.

If Charlene had believed that was the end of her bizarre relationship with Gerald Gallego, she was greatly mistaken. Probably no husband and wife team alive were as bound by blood, sexual perversions, and the deadly secrets between them as these two were. Escape would not come so easily for Charlene.

But for a while anyway, the two drifted apart and neither seemed the worse for it. In late August, Gerald had quit his job at the Argonaut Club and moved out of his apartment.

Accompanied by his pregnant girlfriend, Patty, Gerald left California for a while and went to Oregon. He had since told Charlene about Patty. Why hide it? he thought. It might do Charlene some good to know he had found a real girl with heart.

Naturally, Charlene was jealous. She had every right to be. Jealousy among women was a good thing, he believed. It made them try harder and not get too complacent.

Gerald sent Patty back to California after only a few days. She later claimed that Gallego, who could not find work in Oregon, had told her he planned to pull some holdups and didn't want to get her involved.

Meanwhile, at Gallego's request, a female acquaintance of his spread the word in the Sacramento area that Gerald, alias Stephen Feil, had been killed in an accident. Perhaps this was his attempt to start all over again with a new identity, while severing himself from his murderous past and its potential consequences.

Gallego returned to Sacramento in the fall of 1980, alive and well. On October 7th, he rented an apartment on Bluebird Lane. He told the apartment manager he was a bartender from Oregon.

In spite of their rift, it did not take long for Gerald and Charlene to begin seeing each other again. By November 1, 1980, they were ready to resume their reign of kidnapping, sexual assault, and murder, which had already crossed three states and claimed nine lives.

That evening, the Gallegos picked up the Oldsmobile Cutlass at Charlene's parents' house. Charlene told her parents that she and Gerald were going out to dinner, then to a movie.

If only Charles and Mercedes Williams had known what their daughter and son-in-law really had on the agenda for that night and the early hours of the next morning, they might have had the best chance to avert tragedy.

For all his toughness and long criminal history, Gerald Gallego seemed to have developed a certain amount of respect over the years for Charles and Mercedes Williams that he had for few others, including their daughter. Possibly because of their unwavering support for Charlene, which Gerald never had with his own mother, and certainly not his father. Gerald also likely felt indebted to Charles Williams as a man who had treated him like a son and selflessly used his vast influence to find Gerald one job after another, no questions asked. If anyone could have reached this psychopathic personality in Gallego, the Williams's would have been at the top of the list.

But that was purely speculative thinking that would not change the facts as they were and were soon to be. In reality, Gerald Gallego had used Mercedes and Charles Williams the same way he used their daughter, his own daughter, and just about everyone else that was ever close to him. He was a man who cared only about himself and his gratification. What he wanted, he got. Damn anyone who stood in his way.

"I'm getting that feeling," slurred Gerald to Charlene as the two drove around late that night of November 1, 1980.

They had been drinking much of the night, giving Gerald the courage to act out once more his fantasies of sexual slaves.

But he did not have to be more specific to his partner-in-crime. Charlene knew exactly what "feeling" he was getting. The same feeling he had gotten three other times this year alone; costing five lives, one that had not even begun yet.

And now he was ready to notch another one or two victims on his belt, and once more he wanted Charlene to assist him.

Why couldn't he have stayed in Oregon? she wondered. It was the first chance she'd had in some time to lead a normal life again and Charlene found herself enjoying it more than she had a right to.

But Gerry couldn't leave well enough alone, she thought resentfully. He had to come back and draw her into his sick web of abduction, sexual slavery, and murder.

Maybe she could talk some sense into him for the first time.

"You've had way too much to drink, Gerry," she told him. "Why don't we just call it a night? We can go to your place."

She glanced at him from behind the wheel. He was glaring at her. "And do what?" he scoffed. "I sure as hell can't get what I want from you. Never have! Now, dammit, get me a girl!"

Charlene stared straight ahead and swallowed nervously. When Gerry was like this, there was no room for compromise. Either she obeyed or else.

She drove around aimlessly while Gerald scanned for possible victims.

They first went through Arden Fair, a popular shopping center across the street from a movie theater and a couple of motels. Finding no prospects there, the two drove to a Tower Records parking lot. It was within a stone's throw of the Country Club Plaza where two earlier victims had been abducted.

Charlene, who was still acting as the lure, could not bring herself to sweet talk anyone so near Country Club Plaza. So she bravely returned to the car empty handed. Gerald cursed her out and demanded they—no, she—keep trying.

A tour of the Maverick Club parking lot in North Highlands turned up nothing. By the time they got back to Arden Fair at around one in the morning on November 2nd, Charlene was hoping Gerald would give up his quest.

She should have known by now that her husband was not a man to give up his perverse cravings until they could be appeased.

He spotted a young couple walking down the center of the parking lot, hand in hand. They were the ones, Gerald thought passionlessly. He ordered Charlene to pull into a parking space and, once she did, he hopped out without saying a word. In hand was the .25 caliber Beretta she had purchased for him earlier that year.

Charlene watched helplessly as Gerry approached what she assumed were college coeds. This was the first time a man had ever been involved in the kidnapping. Charlene felt some alarm. Men were not as safe as women; even if threatened by a gun. Maybe he would give Gerry trouble, meaning trouble for her as well.

She had to be prepared to do whatever she had to to protect Gerry. After all, like it or not, in this instance, his best interests were most definitely hers as well.

They had plans, big plans. Indeed, the future had never looked brighter for Craig Miller, twenty-two, and his twenty-one-year-old fiancee, Mary Elizabeth Sowers. The California State University, Sacramento seniors were planning to be married on the last day of 1981 because New Year's Eve was Mary Beth's favorite day.

In the meantime, they seemed to be leading charmed lives. Craig, an honor student, was a member of the Sigma Phi Epsilon fraternity and an accounting executive. Mary Beth, was attractive, bright, outgoing, a finance major, and member of the Alpha Chi Omega sorority. Both were due to graduate in the spring of 1981.

That night they had attended a Sigma Phi Epsilon Founder's Day dinner-dance at the Carousel Restaurant in Arden Fair. As they had become accustomed to, they drew much attention as the all-American couple. Neither took their individual or collective fortunes for granted, yet were modest almost to a fault.

They left the Carousel Restaurant shortly after

midnight and had planned to go straight home. When Craig and Mary Beth saw the portly man approaching them in the parking lot, they never really had a chance to react before they saw the gun staring at them. The man holding it, with a menacing look on his face, said flatly with alcohol on his breath: "Let's go—"

They probably wondered where? Surely this was all a big misunderstanding that could be straightened out? Even a robbery, under the circumstances, would not be too bad.

Fearing the deadly power of a gun if used, Mary Beth and Craig played out their captor's game, no doubt expecting an outcome they could all live with. But certainly not die for.

They underestimated Gerald Gallego and his motives. It would prove to be a fatal miscalculation.

It was nearly one-thirty in the morning when Craig Miller's fraternity brother left the Founder's Day celebration. Walking through the parking lot with his date, the fraternity brother recognized Craig and Mary Beth sitting in the back seat of a silver Oldsmobile Cutlass. The headlights were on and the motor running.

Given that the fraternity brother knew Miller and Sowers had driven there in Mary Beth's bright red Honda and the Oldsmobile was unfamiliar, he was curious as to what was going on.

The fraternity brother left his date standing and approached the Oldsmobile. He opened the driver's side door and leaned his tall and husky frame into the empty driver's seat to talk with his friends. It was then that he noticed the somewhat intimidating presence of the stocky man up front in the passenger seat. The man glared but said nothing.

The fraternity brother faced Craig and Mary Beth in the back. Both looked tense.

"Thought you two had enough partying for one night?" said the fraternity brother, half joking.

Craig was not laughing as he said to him: "Get the hell out of here. This is no place for you."

If Craig was hoping his fraternity brother would read between the lines, it worked. The fraternity brother sensed all was not right. Only before he could figure out exactly what was wrong, he was accosted by someone outside the car.

"What the hell do you think you're doing in my car!"

The fraternity brother lifted out and was surprised to see the boisterous voice coming from a short, pregnant, blonde-haired woman. She acted as if he had committed a federal offense. Why?

"Who are you, anyway?" he asked her, baffled. "What's going on here?"

"None of your damned business," she spat at him. "You bastard; don't ever put your filthy ass in my car again!" Then she slapped him hard.

It certainly caught his attention, even from a woman so small and fragile looking. He did not appreciate being hit, and told her so.

She yelled some more expletives at him that were definitely unladylike, got into the car, and screeched away.

But not before the fraternity brother, still pissed at the woman and worried about Craig and Mary Beth, took down the license plate number of the Oldsmobile.

Charlene had reacted to the large friend, she presumed, of those in the back seat with unaccustomed rancor. It was all she could think of to get him away from the car before the two back there did any real talking. Her crazy woman act had worked. He could have spoiled everything, she thought. Gerry might have had to kill them all right there on the spot.

It would have attracted others. Then what might have happened? Maybe they would have overpowered us. Then we would be arrested and all hell would break loose. Especially if the cops knew what she knew.

The thought of spending the rest of her life in prison terrified Charlene. Even more frightening was being given a death sentence. Execution. What a horrible way to die . . .

But they were not out of the woods yet, her mind told her as she pulled out of the Arden Fair parking lot and onto the street. That boy, who had stuck his nose where it was definitely not wanted, seemed to be writing something down when she sped off. Common sense told her it was the license plate number of her car.

Her license plate number!

It would be traced to her father. Then to her.

How the hell would she explain it to her parents? She certainly couldn't begin to tell them the whole story. Daddy's little girl would never be involved in the murder of nine human beings—soon to be eleven.

Maybe the man-sized boy had misread the plate, she hoped. She certainly hadn't given him much time to work with. For all she knew, he was just jotting down something entirely innocent to perhaps give to the girl he was with.

Instinctively, Charlene suspected her first guess was right. She brought it up to Gerry, who had been remarkably calm during the whole ordeal.

He seemed to take her fears in stride. "You think the cops will believe some punk?"

Why not? Charlene thought. He had seen the two college kids in the back seat. He knew them.

He was a witness, the first one in all this time. He could identify us as their abductors.

Only Gerry was too drunk to see that. His sloppiness and desperation to find a girl had gone too far this time, sensed Charlene. She was sure the axe was about to drop on both of them.

"Get on 50," directed Gerald. "Go east."

Charlene obeyed, soon entering U.S. 50. Traffic was very light at this time of morning. Charlene was thankful for that much. They didn't need any other "witnesses."

"Do you two have names?" Gerald asked his captives, the .25 still pointed towards the back seat.

"Mary Beth Sowers," said the girl politely.

"Craig Miller," the boy said in less than friendly terms.

Charlene glanced in the rearview mirror at him. She thought he was nice looking. Better looking, in fact, than Gerry, whose heavy drinking and general disregard for his appearance these days left him fat and very unattractive.

She peeked again at the boy and this time felt anger towards him. It was his fault that they hadn't left the parking lot sooner. He had thrown some car keys out the window and Gerry made her go look for them, which she never found.

That was when the big brute showed up and she gave him a piece of her mind and the taste of her hand across his face. She'd also had a choice word or two for the boy in back. What was he thinking in doing such a stupid thing? Did he honestly think that would make one damned bit of difference in his ultimate fate?

Gerald asked Craig Miller if he had any money. The boy said not much, maybe ten dollars at best. Gerald demanded his wallet and frowned when he saw that Craig Miller had not underestimated his current net worth.

Looking hard at Mary Beth, Gerald hissed: "What are you doing with a bum like this?"

Mary Beth did not answer.

Gerald mumbled some expletives before looking at the highway and directing Charlene to get off at the Bass Lake Road exit.

Charlene turned off the highway and drove until Gerald told her to stop in the middle of a gravel road near Bass Lake in El Dorado County.

"You want him?" Gerry asked her, and indicated Craig Miller with the gun.

Was he serious? Charlene thought, and glanced at the boy, who looked understandably tense. If the circumstances had been different, she and Craig Miller might have made a nice couple. In fact, she thought, if only a lot of circumstances had been different, she would not even be in that car right now.

She favored her husband and answered firmly: "No, Gerry, I don't."

Gerald shrugged. "Can't say I never asked." He told Craig Miller to get out.

Craig gazed at Mary Beth regrettably, as if he knew it would be for the last time. Earlier he had asked the kidnappers to let her go and do what they wanted with him. The man with the gun had laughed and said, "You'd like that, wouldn't you? Not a chance!"

Craig had even thrown Mary Beth's car keys out the window in a move designed to buy time—or at worst—let others know that they had been abducted.

Craig Miller had run out of options as he exited the car. His one hope was that they would leave him out there in the middle of nowhere. Surely they would not kill him, or Mary Beth, for ten lousy bucks?

Gerald told Craig Miller to start walking. Craig had not taken more than two steps towards the front of the car when Gerald shot him point blank in the back of the head.

Mary Beth was forced to watch in horror as Craig went down. Gerald Gallego now stood over his fallen victim and fired two more shots into his head.

He left the corpse where it lay and climbed into the back seat with Mary Beth. "Take us to my apartment," he ordered Charlene.

She began driving, still shivering from witnessing Gerry execute that boy right before her very eyes. Gerry had always done his dirty work out of

181

her sight—or at least the worst parts. Now he had reached the point in his lunacy and brutality where he wanted Charlene to see what a monster he had become. It was almost as if he was warning her that no matter who pulled the trigger, they were both equally guilty.

She would do well to remember that.

TWENTY

The jealous side of Charlene could not help but be irked by the sexual embraces she saw Gerald engaged in with Mary Beth Sowers. Charlene's view was limited to the rearview mirror as she approached Gerald's apartment, but as far as she was concerned she had seen all she cared to.

She knew that Gerry putting his hands all over Mary Beth was totally involuntary on her part. In Charlene's mind, though, this conflicted with her seeing Mary Beth as a young and beautiful woman, wearing a stunning purple silk evening gown and, obviously, turning on Gerry in a way she had not been able to for some time.

"You're going to be my Krista tonight," Charlene listened to Gerald coo to his sex slave in the back seat. "You want to be my Krista?"

Mary Beth did not offer a response.

Once they reached the apartment, an irritated Charlene watched as Gerry took Mary Beth Sowers into the bedroom, closing the door behind them. Charlene padded and pouted her way to the living room where she lay on the sofa and waited for Gerry to get it over with and get her, Mary Beth, the hell out of that apartment.

How did he expect her to ever want to make love in that bed again? muttered Charlene to herself.

She could hear Gerry and his sex slave arguing—or was his slave pleading with him? and other noises that sounded like the headboard knocking against the wall. It did not take much imagination for Charlene to know what Gerald was forcing his captive to endure.

Several hours had passed before Gerald and Mary Beth emerged from the bedroom. Charlene had drifted in and out of sleep and was somewhere in between when Gerry slapped her into consciousness.

"The party's over," he told her. "Time to take Ms. Coed for a ride."

Charlene yawned and stared at Mary Beth. Her dress and hair were disheveled, makeup smeared from tears, and she appeared to be completely exhausted and scared to death.

Suddenly she no longer looked like a girl with

heart, Krista, or anyone else that Charlene had reason to be jealous of.

Charlene drove with Gerald beside her and Mary Beth in the back seat. Gerald kept an eye on his victim, the .25 caliber in hand, and instructed Charlene to take I-80 and drive towards Reno.

By now Charlene was able to operate almost on automatic. Gerald had trained her well. His commands were rarely challenged or disobeyed.

They got off the interstate near Sierra College in Placer County. Charlene drove to the end of an isolated road where Gerry took Mary Beth into a pasture. Charlene waited in the car for the inevitable. It happened.

She heard the familiar pops of gunfire—three to be exact—and knew that the girl named Mary Beth Sowers was dead, or close to it.

What Charlene did not know was that Mary Beth's tragic ending would help galvanize a horrified community and bring together law enforcement agencies to ultimately capture the coed and her fiance's killers.

When Gerald returned to the car, he had a smile on his face as if patting himself on the back for a job well done. But it was not yet complete.

They drove back to the apartment and went through the well-practiced ritual of cleaning, wiping, disposing of possible evidence that could be used against them.

In Gerald's mind, this was a mere precautionary formality. Charlene, however, saw this as a bad omen. Perhaps this time no amount of scrubbing and disappearing acts would save them.

Around 9 A.M. on Sunday, November 2, 1980, Craig Miller's fraternity brother and several other worried friends of the missing coeds returned to the Arden Fair parking lot in search of Mary Beth's red Honda. The fraternity brother had had a sleepless night, concerned that Miller and Sowers might have been the victims of foul play.

The group located the Honda, still parked where the couple had left it. It was unlocked. Mary Beth's expensive cashmere coat was on the front seat. A further search and Mary Beth's car keys were discovered underneath the car.

Now all doubts were erased. The fraternity brother knew something terrible had happened to Craig and Mary Beth. He locked the car and the group went to see the police to report their friends as missing.

Meanwhile, Craig Miller's mother became alarmed when her son failed to show up at his job for his 10 A.M. shift that Sunday morning. She, too, notified the police and the search was on for the normally dependable and careful couple.

Detective Lee Taylor, assigned to the missing persons squad for the Sacramento Police Department, ran a trace with the Department of Motor Vehicles on the license number the fraternity brother had scribbled down of the Oldsmobile. Charles Williams was listed as the legal owner of the 1977 Oldsmobile Cutlass in which Craig Miller and Mary Beth Sowers were last seen alive. Williams's daughter, Charlene A. Williams, was the registered owner.

It was time for the detective to pay a visit to the Williams home.

Charlene and Gerald were up and at it with little sleep that morning. Though they had yet to have any reason to panic, both were on edge and anxious to clear up any remaining loose ends to their early morning kidnapping and murder of the co-eds. The weapon used to kill Craig and Mary Beth, her purse and its contents, and anything else conceivable that might provide a clue that Mary Beth had been sexually violated in that very apartment hours earlier, had to vanish completely.

The Gallegos took the evidence and drove to a place eerily called Miller Park, near the Sacramento River. When the coast was clear, Gerald threw the evidence into the river, where it would never be found by anyone.

Charlene probably wondered how Gerald could be so reckless, especially with his last four victims, in his abductions and killings, yet be so intense and careful when trying to distance himself from his brutalities.

Gerald and Charlene went to her parents' house, entering through the back door. They were met almost immediately by Charlene's mother, Mercedes Williams. Quietly, while looking befuddled, she told them the police were there.

"Damn!" muttered Gallego almost to himself. "I'd better get the hell outta here." He furrowed his brow at Charlene. "Better go see what they want. Don't say anything we'll regret. I'll call later." And he was back out the door.

Charlene became physically ill, vomiting in the kitchen sink. Her mother thought it was because of her pregnancy. Charlene knew it was the mounting pressures of what they had done. It all seemed to be coming down around them.

"What's going on, Charlene?" her mother asked with apprehension in her face.

Charlene, having recovered somewhat from the initial shock, batted her lashes and said innocently: "I have no idea."

"They thought you might have been kidnapped, Charlene," Mercedes said in disbelief.

Charlene gave her a look of stupefaction. "I don't know why the hell they would think that. Who would want to kidnap me?"

Charlene followed her mother into the living room where her father was seated along with two

detectives. She was introduced to Detectives Lee
Taylor and Larry Burchett.

"How can I help you?" Charlene asked them politely.

They told her about the missing coeds, Craig
Miller and Mary Beth Sowers, the fraternity brother
who had been slapped by a young woman and
later took down the license plate number of a car
she was driving with Miller and Sowers in back—
a car that was registered to a Charlene Adell Williams.

Charlene could have cracked here and there, but
kept her cool just as she had twice before when
interviewed by Detective Trujillo. Obviously, the
detectives had no real proof of anything or they
would have arrested her right there on the spot.

She told them that she knew nothing about the
disappearance of the college students. She and her
boyfriend, Stephen, had gone to see a movie last
night and had returned to his apartment around
midnight and stayed the night.

Everything about Charlene Williams was believable. Her tiny, slender, sweet-looking appearance
gave her almost instant credibility. And she was
several months pregnant. Pregnant women did not
abduct people, much less harm them. Yet the detectives also had that license number and a description of the car and driver, which happened to fit
her to a T.

What were you wearing last night? they asked.

The same clothing she wore now, she told them, which was a pair of jeans and a T-shirt. She added that the T-shirt replaced a pink maternity smock she had worn until she got sick all over it due to her pregnancy, and changed it at her boyfriend's house.

There was still the question of the Oldsmobile the fraternity brother had seen Sowers and Miller drive off in.

Charlene nearly panicked. She said, without thinking, that she and her boyfriend had taken his red Triumph to the movie and back.

When the suspicious detectives informed her that the Triumph had been parked in the street outside her parents' home for several days, Charlene knew she had to think—quickly. They were watching her like a hawk. One false move or wrong word and they would know she was lying and it would be all over for her and Gerry.

So Charlene went with the tried and true story that had worked so well with Detective Trujillo. In her sweetest voice, she apologized for the confusion and confessed that she had gotten so drunk last night that she couldn't remember which car they took. Nevertheless, she told them steadfastly that she never saw the missing students.

It was possible she was being truthful, the detectives considered. But they were still not entirely comfortable..

They asked for permission to search Charlene's Oldsmobile. She granted it easily. Why not? she thought. They wouldn't find anything. She and Gerry had seen to that by giving it an A to Z cleaning job.

Charlene accompanied the detectives to her car, which was parked in the driveway. She handed one of them the keys and watched in silence as they looked inside and out, hoping to find anything that might be incriminating.

A shred of doubt went through Charlene's mind. What if she and Gerry had missed something? Would they find it? Would there be more questions to try and trip her up?

Damn you, Gerry, she cursed within. You've put us in this mess with your stupid, careless insistence on finding a girl last night. Why did you have to choose that one—and her boyfriend?

The detectives seemed satisfied at the moment with Charlene's story. They had found no physical evidence in the car to indicate that there had been a struggle or that a crime had been committed in it.

Next, the detectives took down information on the red Triumph Charlene said belonged to her boyfriend. When they began to ask her more questions, Charlene conveniently became ill. It was morning sickness, she told them, adding that she was seven months pregnant, in case they didn't have eyes. Also the effects of a hangover were bothering her. She would be glad to provide more information if she could when she recovered from her ills.

Under the circumstances, the detectives had no other choice but to cut the interview short. They told Charlene they would return later that day to take a photograph of her. Charlene assured them she would be happy to cooperate.

Once the detectives left, Charlene knew she had to face the inquiring minds of her parents.

"What the hell have you gotten yourself into, Charlene?" Charles Williams asked his daughter. Even that rare outburst from Charlene's father reflected more his concern for her well-being. If there was anything Charles Williams could have done to get this straightened out on behalf of his beloved daughter, he would have.

But not even daddy could pull enough strings to get Charlene out of the deep hole she had dug for herself this time. And she knew it, sinking ever so deeply with each passing moment.

"It's all just a big mistake," she told her parents softly. "It'll all be straightened out. You'll see."

Back at the police station, Detectives Taylor and Burchett ran a check on the license number of the

Triumph. It belonged to a Stephen Robert Feil. The detectives got a copy of Feil's driver's license. Craig Miller's fraternity brother identified the driver's license photograph of Stephen Feil as the man in the front seat of the Oldsmobile Cutlass while Craig and Mary Beth sat in the back.

The detectives went to Stephen Feil aka Gerald Gallego's apartment. To their disappointment, the suspect was not there. They left a note for him to call them as soon as he returned.

It was four-thirty in the afternoon when the detectives made a return visit to the home of Charles and Mercedes Williams. They had hoped to take Charlene to the station to be photographed. The Williamses informed the detectives that their daughter was not home but would be back at eight for dinner.

When questioned about Stephen Feil, Charles Williams admitted that Charlene was married to Feil and that he was the father of the baby she was carrying.

The interview was interrupted when the detectives heard a message on their police radio. Craig Miller's body had been found near Bass Lake. The college senior had been shot three times in the head.

The detectives informed the Williamses of this distressing news, while urging them to have Charlene call them as soon as she arrived.

The whereabouts of Mary Beth Sowers was still unknown.

Gerald and Charlene were beginning to feel the heat. Each blamed the other for the predicament they were in. If only you had contained your sexual desires, pouted Charlene. Gerald countered with: If you hadn't told the cops anything, they'd have nothing to tie us to any crime.

Gerald figured if he and Charlene went back and found Craig Miller's body and put it somewhere where no one else would stumble upon it, at least there wouldn't be anything left for the cops to use against them.

That evening of November 2nd, the Gallegos attempted to retrace the path they had taken when they kidnapped Craig Miller and Mary Beth Sowers. U.S. 50 East to Bass Lake Road. They stopped in an area on a gravel road where Charlene was positive Craig Miller had met his death. Only there was no body to be found.

Was her mind playing tricks on her? This was the place where Gerry had shot that boy three times!

But it can't be, she thought. Otherwise he'd still be here, wouldn't he? The police couldn't have found him already?

Unknown to the Gallegos was that the authorities had in fact gotten there before them. Leaving

Craig Miller's body just off the side of the road to be easily discovered would prove to be the murderous couple's undoing.

"Where the hell is he?" shouted Gerald at his wife.

"I don't know!" she shouted back.

"Are you sure it was here?"

"I don't know," she repeated, this time more timidly.

They both noted signs that the ground around them looked different than they remembered. There were footprints going every which way, tire tracks, cigarette butts—as if others had recently been over the area.

"Dammit to hell!" cursed Gerald. "They must have found him! We've gotta get out of town, and fast!"

"And go where?" Charlene had not been prepared to become a fugitive. How could they survive? How long would they have to be gone?

"Don't ask questions I can't answer," growled Gerald. "I need time to think and I sure as hell can't do it here! Now let's get outta here," he ordered, "unless you want to have that baby in prison!"

Charlene got the message. They were in big trouble, regardless of whose fault it was. If the police knew about one victim, then they would probably learn about another . . . and another . . . She had already lost one baby. She wouldn't be forced to give this one up too!

Charlene decided right then that her only real choice at this point was to stand by her man. Gerry would somehow find a way to protect her.

In the meantime, they had to stick together as any man and wife should.

Later that night, Charlene telephoned her mother and told her in that innocent-nothing-to-hide voice that she had mastered so well: "Gerry and I just decided to play pinball instead of coming over for dinner. Sorry. I'll call you tomorrow. And, don't worry!"

She felt she had enough to worry about for her and her parents, not to mention Gerry.

It was 6 P.M. on November 2nd, when Detectives Burchett and Taylor went to the Arden Fair parking lot and made arrangements to have Mary Beth Sowers's Honda impounded.

Later, the detectives learned that some Bass Lake area residents had reported to El Dorado County authorities that they heard three gunshots between seven and seven-thirty that morning.

An autopsy performed on Craig Miller determined that the young man had been shot once above the right ear, once by the right cheekbone, and once at the back of the neck—all at point-blank range.

On November 3rd, Charles Williams, perhaps sensing that his daughter was in real trouble, largely because of her involvement with Gerald Gallego, phoned the detectives and told them that Stephen Feil's real name was Gerald Gallego. Williams said that the alias was used because Gerald had an arrest warrant out for him in Butte County on charges of incest and other sex offenses.

Ironically, the real Stephen Feil turned out to be a California State Police officer who claimed no knowledge of Gerald Gallego. Charlene believed Feil to be a distant cousin whose identity she was perfectly willing to allow Gerald Gallego to borrow.

Charles Williams's disclosure helped give investigators a clearer picture of just what and who they were up against. Not only did they learn of the charges Gallego faced in Butte County, but also that he had an extensive criminal history dating back to when he was six years old, including convictions for robbery and theft and allegations of numerous sex crimes.

Given that Charlene Gallego had no record of criminal wrongdoing, detectives must have wondered how she possibly could have ended up with a man like Gerald Gallego.

One thing that was abundantly clear to detectives by now was that the Gallegos were the number one suspects in the kidnapping and murder of

Craig Miller and believed abduction of Mary Beth Sowers.

The one real question left at this point was who would authorities find first, Mary Beth Sowers or Charlene and Gerald Gallego?

Both appeared to be only a matter of time.

TWENTY-ONE

Whatever Charles and Mercedes Williams may have thought about the nature of the trouble their daughter and son-in-law were in, their loyalty to Charlene remained unwavering. The Williamses were willing to risk criminal prosecution to help their daughter in any way they could.

On the evening of November 3, 1980, Charles and Mercedes Williams agreed to meet Charlene and Gerald in a parking lot in Fair Oaks, one of the many neighboring suburban towns bordering Sacramento.

Charlene hated getting her parents involved in this. But she also knew that at this stage they were the only ones she and Gerry could trust, and count on for needed funds.

Gerald also viewed the Williamses participation

with some regret. The incest charges were one thing. This Miller situation was much more serious. He didn't really want to bring them down over this. But what other choice did he and Charlene have?

Even if he had wanted to call his own mother, the police were probably watching her. There was no need to cause her more grief. Or his daughter, whom he still cared for in spite of everything else.

The parking lot was mostly deserted when the Williamses and Gallegos met at one end.

"We're just going to leave for a while," Gerald explained.

"Why don't you turn yourselves in?" urged Charles Williams. "If this is all a mistake, I'm sure we can get it cleared up."

"It's too late for that," scoffed Gerald, a cigarette dangling from a corner of his mouth. "You see, they need a scapegoat for this Miller murder. They'll somehow try to use that Butte County warrant to try and make me a killer. I, we, can't stick around and let that happen."

Mercedes regarded her only child. "You both don't have to go, Charlene," she suggested. "You haven't done anything. Why not let Gerry go somewhere by himself until things cool down."

"He's my husband," Charlene said, aware that she had a far greater role in this than her parents could ever imagine in their worst nightmares. "I've got to go where he goes. I'm sorry."

"So am I," her mother spoke softly.

Charles Williams likely respected and admired his daughter's courage and loyalty, but he had to be equally concerned in saying goodbye to his precious daughter under adverse circumstances.

Charlene kissed her parents and assured them that the police would soon find the real killer of Craig Miller. Then they could return and their lives would be back to normal.

In reality, Charlene knew that whatever happened henceforth, life would never be normal for her again.

The Williamses gave them some money and warm clothing they had hurriedly gathered for the couple. As they saw the Gallegos drive off in the Oldsmobile, Charles Williams must have wondered if he would ever see his little girl again.

The Federal Bureau of Investigation had joined in on the search for the fugitive couple after it became clear that the Gallegos had crossed state lines in order to escape capture. The federal fugitive warrant charged the couple with unlawful flight to avoid prosecution.

The FBI would play a critical role in the apprehension of the Gallegos.

The forces of the law were closing in on Gerald and Charlene Gallego, but for a time they must have truly believed they could evade the authorities indefinitely. After all, they had for more than two years.

The Gallegos drove the Oldsmobile east down Highway 50. They were headed towards the Sierras again as they had so often done during their twenty-six-month reign of abduction, rape, and death. They were headed towards Reno via Lake Tahoe and Carson City. Neither said much about the sequence of events that had led up to this unknown journey. Charlene knew all along that sooner or later it would all catch up to them. Now it nearly had.

Gerald, on the other hand, felt confident that even if they were caught the police had nothing they could make stick. As long as Charlene kept her mouth shut, neither of them had too much to worry about.

Of course, he could always kill her here and now, Gerald considered. It would be easy enough to strangle the life out of her small neck and dump her off in the mountains. That way there would be no one who could finger him in the death of Craig Miller, Mary Beth Sowers, or anyone else. He sure as hell would not admit to a damned thing.

He glanced at his unusually quiet and pregnant wife. She was scared, he could tell. He saw at that moment the sweet, vulnerable girl he had first laid eyes on at the Black Stallion Card Room. Then she had been a girl with heart. Maybe she still was, he admitted.

But he could never tell her that. It was too late for him to grow soft now. Women, whether they admitted it or not, liked men who were tough, macho, strong-willed.

Any thoughts about killing Charlene left Gerald as they approached Reno.

Back in Sacramento, investigators had discovered bullets in the attic of a tavern where Gallego had worked as a bartender. Gerald had fired the shots into the ceiling to show off in front of a pretty lady.

Ballistics tests matched the bullets with the ones taken from Craig Miller's corpse. The evidence against Gallego was mounting as the search for him and his wife, Charlene, continued.

In Reno, the Gallegos dumped the car in the Circus-Circus casino hotel parking lot. "It's too hot to keep driving," realized Gerald. "Probably every damn cop in the country is on the lookout for a silver Cutlass."

Charlene, at Gerald's direction, phoned her parents from the casino and told them where to find the car.

Then, perhaps on her own initiative in an attempt to dissuade those pursuing them, Charlene phoned a Sacramento attorney who had represented her parents.

After identifying herself, Charlene told him succinctly: "I'm traveling with my husband. Neither of us knows anything about those college kids who disappeared."

The attorney seemed genuinely interested and wanted to hear more. But Charlene, who knew Gerry was outside waiting, was able to provide few details. She had probably already told him too much, she thought.

The attorney had suggested they give themselves up on Thursday, two days later. He would do all he could to help them.

She told him she would discuss it with Gerry and call him back.

That discussion never took place.

By the time the police found the Gallegos' abandoned car in the Circus-Circus lot, the suspects were long gone.

The Gallegos took a Greyhound bus to Salt Lake City, Utah. To other riders they must have seemed like a typical young couple with children, mortgage payments, and dreams of growing old together.

No one could have imagined that beneath their normal facades lay fugitives from justice and crimes that would shock the country.

In Salt Lake City, Charlene called her parents for money, which was running in short supply. Gerald had insisted upon it. Just keep the call brief, he told her. You never know who might be listening.

"We need the money to come home," Charlene lied as Gerry had instructed her to.

The Williamses wired $500 to a Western Union office in Salt Lake City.

Gerald and Charlene used the money to stay on the run. From Utah they traveled to Denver. From there they made their way to Omaha, Nebraska.

The tension and stress must have been at an all-time high for the couple, who were used to being the hunters rather than the hunted. Even Gerald, a hardened criminal by every standard, had placed himself in an unenviable position where possible danger lurked behind every corner. Charlene, who may have once considered her bizarre relationship with Gerald an adventure, had to now have some inkling of the fear her husband's sex slaves must have felt.

Once again, the Gallegos' money dwindled to nearly nothing. Charlene went to the well one time too many, phoning her parents to beg for money.

"I'll never ask you for anything again," she promised weakly. "Just send enough to get us back to Sacramento."

The Williamses reluctantly agreed, sending another $500 to their daughter via Western Union. Only this time they decided if Charlene was to have any chance to get out of this alive, they had to betray her for her own good.

Charles and Mercedes Williams notified the FBI that they had wired the funds to Omaha.

Unbeknownst to the Williamses, they had been under around-the-clock surveillance by FBI agents and members of the Sacramento Police Department ever since their daughter had fled the state.

Using unmarked cars, agents followed Charles and Mercedes Williams as they left their home on Saturday, November 15th. Charlene's parents drove to Sparks, Nevada. On November 16th, the Williamses were observed entering a Western Union office in Sparks.

Afterwards, agents learned from Charles and Mercedes Williams that they had just sent $500 to their daughter in Omaha.

The information was relayed to the FBI's Omaha field office and the beginning of the end had begun for the Gallegos.

Gerald and Charlene had checked in at the Hill Town Inn in Omaha on Friday, November 14th, as Mr. and Mrs. Stephen Galloway. They listed Chico, California as their hometown. They spent the next three days keeping a low profile in their eight dollar a day room, eating mostly in the motel's restaurant.

On Monday morning, November 17, 1980, the Gallegos had breakfast, then headed over to the

Western Union office in downtown Omaha. It was to be a routine pickup of money the couple believed would come indefinitely from Charlene's parents who, after all, had always come through for them in the past.

Even then, Gerald was not taking anything for granted. He knew the inherent danger in having Charlene's parents send too much and being too knowledgeable of their whereabouts. He had talked to Charlene about possibly finding a job in Omaha and staying there for a while. At least until after the baby was born.

It seemed like a perfect plan to Gerald. Who would ever find them in Omaha, Nebraska of all places?

FBI agents were stationed in and around the Western Union office, waiting for sight or sound of the Gallegos. At 11:30 A.M., the fugitive couple appeared. Neither showed signs of nervousness or fear as they approached the Western Union office.

At the last moment, almost as if he had an inkling of trouble, Gerald Gallego suddenly parted from his wife and began walking down the street. FBI agents, shotguns ready for a man believed to be possibly armed and extremely dangerous, trailed the suspect in a car.

Charlene, unaware of the surveillance on them, waited until Gerald had rounded the corner before entering the Western Union office. She calmly stepped up to the counter, identified herself as Charlene Gallego, and asked if any money had come in for her.

At that point, FBI agent Harlan Phillips walked up to Charlene and queried tersely: "Charlene?"

She turned and responded involuntarily: "Yes . . . ?"

"FBI!" said Phillips sharply to the short, seven months pregnant suspect. "You are under arrest on an unlawful flight to avoid prosecution on a murder charge!"

Charlene offered no resistance and actually seemed almost relieved that it was over as she was handcuffed. An order to "take Gallego" was then radioed to the agents following him.

The car carrying FBI agents pulled alongside the suspect. Three agents—two with shotguns aimed and ready—sprang from the car and ordered Gerald Gallego to raise his hands.

One might have expected Gallego—a career criminal who had viciously murdered at least ten people—to go down swinging or at least shooting. After all, he had vowed to Charlene that he would never be taken alive. Had he made even the slightest wrong move, the agents would have undoubtedly obliged his desire.

Instead, Gerald Gallego proved to be far more cowardly when it came to his own life than the life he had taken from others. He raised his arms and was taken into custody without the slightest resistance.

Surprisingly, neither Gerald nor Charlene were armed at the time of their arrest. It was probably one of the few times in his adult life (when he was not incarcerated) that Gerald Gallego did not have a firearm in his possession. If he had, the outcome might have been very different.

As it was, the Gallegos' destructive path of child molestation, sexual assault, stark unrelenting fear, violence, and murder had come to an undramatic halt. For the families of their victims, their nightmares would have to be relived over and over before their loved ones could finally be put to rest.

On November 22, 1980, five days after the arrest of Gerald and Charlene Gallego, the body of Mary Elizabeth Sowers was discovered in a shallow trench in a Placer County pasture. The twenty-one-year-old college senior—still wearing the purplish-blue silk evening gown that had the young men swooning at the Sigma Phi Epsilon Founder's Day dinner-dance nearly three weeks earlier—had been bound and shot three times in the head.

Mary Beth was buried beside her fiance, Craig Miller. The couple's death would not be in vain, as it resulted in the capture and conviction of their abductors before the Gallegos could seek out and murder any other unsuspecting victims.

TWENTY-TWO

"**G**erald A. Gallego admitted killing a young Sacramento college couple," prosecutor James Morris said in his opening statement before the jury in the murder trial of the accused, Gerald Armond Gallego, in the deaths of Craig Miller and Mary Beth Sowers.

The trial began in November 1982, and would pit Morris against Gallego himself. The defendant either had an enormous amount of self-confidence or was making the biggest mistake of his life, to date.

Presiding over the trial was Judge Norman Spellberg. A jury of seven women and five men would decide the fate of a man whose own wife (or so he wanted to believe) was fully prepared to testify against him in the Miller-Sowers murders and nine

others. Gerald Gallego had put forth his best effort
to block Charlene's testimony on the grounds of
spousal privilege. He had gone out of his way to
marry her twice for this very reason.

The trouble was, in Gallego's haste to marry one
woman after another (which totaled five before
Charlene ever entered the picture), he had failed to
legally divorce wife number two. Thus both marriages to Charlene and her three predecessors were
illegal and invalid.

Charlene Adell Gallego was now Charlene Adell
Williams again, much to the chagrin of Gerald. In
denying his last attempt to suppress Charlene's obviously damaging testimony, the California Supreme Court ruled without comment to Gallego's
petition in January of 1983. This effectively cleared
the way for Charlene to testify against the man she
believed she had legally married, and who was the
father of her nearly two-year-old son, Gerry, Jr.

Prosecutor Morris revealed to the jury in his
opening statement that Gallego's "confession" occurred during "lawfully monitored" jailhouse conversations with his mother-in-law, Mercedes
Williams, and a former girlfriend.

"I had no idea I'd do something like this," Gallego was quoted as saying to his ex-girlfriend in
early December 1980. "I'm going to try to prove I
was strictly out of my mind in court."

A day later, Morris told the court that Gallego

said to Mercedes Williams:

"What it's boiling down to, mom, is my defense will be a diminished capacity. I was on LSD ... Because I was under the influence ... hopefully would give me a second [degree murder sentence], which would be about fifteen years ... I would take fifteen years in a minute."

Morris went on to say that a smug Gallego told the ex-girlfriend: "The only thing they can prove for a fact is that it was my gun that did it [shot Miller and Sowers], and they were in my car that night ... and that we [Gerald and Charlene] ran."

The prosecutor built up the vulnerability of his star witness, Charlene Williams, telling the jury that Gerald Gallego dominated his wife, who was ten years his junior, from the time they first met in 1977. Morris described Charlene as "five feet tall, barely one hundred pounds." Gallego played his other girlfriends off against her, the prosecutor said, to induce her to prove her love for him.

Morris then went into the nature of Gallego's "sexual fantasy," which was to "kidnap a young girl, or any girl, and take her as captive to some location," where he sexually assaulted her for his pleasure.

"If she [Charlene] had any guts or had any heart," Morris alleged Gallego told Charlene, "she would help him fulfill his fantasy."

James Morris's opening statement lasted two and

a half hours and, no doubt, was his attempt to stack the jury against Gallego from the outset, while siding with Charlene.

In a puzzling move, Gallego, the attorney, chose to defer his opening statement until after Morris had completed his. Once the damage had been done—and it had—it would prove impossible for the inexperienced (in legal terms) Gallego to undo it. Not that he had much of a case to begin with.

Amongst the State's thirty witnesses, one of the more damaging to Gerald Gallego was his mother-in-law, Mercedes Williams. Distraught and teary-eyed during much of her testimony, Mrs. Williams revealed to the jury how she helped her daughter and Gallego elude the authorities for more than two weeks before helping them nab the fugitive couple.

Mercedes Williams also told (in corroborating Morris's opening statement) of the jailhouse conversations between her and Gerald Gallego. In those conversations, Gallego allegedly implicated himself in the kidnapping-murders of Craig Miller and Mary Beth Sowers in an attempt to mount a defense.

According to Mercedes Williams, Gallego showed her a handwritten note, through the window of the visiting room at the Sacramento County Jail, that said: "Charlene will know the story when

I see her. Say nothing [to her attorney at the time] until I see her."

Mrs. Williams claimed that Gallego tore up the note after she read it.

Upon the conclusion of Mercedes Williams's testimony on direct, Gerald Gallego bit into his lip, quivered in his chair at the defense table, and took a long pause before muttering: "Judge, I don't have any questions for this witness."

Once again, Gallego had hurt his own case by making a wrong move in his defense, albeit one that showed his continued respect for his mother-in-law even under these circumstances. By passing up the chance to cross-examine Mercedes Williams, he had let one of the prosecution's most important witnesses off the hook.

Clearly, the People's case against Gallego rested largely on the slender shoulders of the prosecution's chief witness, Charlene Gallego, who was now legally Charlene Williams again. Her testimony was easily the most anticipated part of a trial that figured to last for months.

Charlene wore a white, lacy Victorian blouse and black skirt as she was escorted into the courtroom on January 10, 1983, to testify against Gerald Gallego. Her demure appearance belied the woman who had willingly participated in the abduction and murder of ten people, including a pregnant woman. Accompanying Charlene into court was her attorney, Hamilton Hintz, Jr., and a Sacramento County Sheriff's deputy.

During a three hour and fifteen minute direct examination by prosecutor James Morris, Charlene nervously detailed the saga of her relationship with Gerald Gallego, including tales of mental and physical abuse, wickedly bizarre sexual fantasies, and cold-blooded murder.

She glanced only occasionally at Gallego during her testimony, except when she told the jury of her feelings towards the other women he saw and the 1978 abortion he forced her to endure. In these instances, Charlene hit Gallego with a hard and hateful stare.

She testified that the purpose of the kidnapping of Miller and Sowers was to fulfill Gallego's "sexual fantasies," which Charlene first learned about in 1978.

When asked what her role was in these fantasies, Charlene testified: "I was to act as a lure, to strike up a conversation with a young girl. She had to be very young and pretty, to coax her outside, such as from a shopping center or mall, outside to our vehicle. From that point on, she would belong to Gerry. He would have her captive to fulfill his fantasies."

"What did you think of Gerald's fantasy?" she was asked.

"I thought he was crazy."

But, Charlene added, she was in love with Gerry and took part in his "competition for real love" because she was to be "this girl with heart that really loved him; she would do anything for him and didn't have to be told what to do."

Charlene told the jury that on November 1, 1980, Gallego announced that "he was getting that feeling," indicating that he wanted her to find a girl for him.

Prosecutor Morris asked the witness if she said no or argued with Gallego.

"No," she responded concisely, and glanced at the man she twice thought of as her husband, "you don't say no to Gerry."

Charlene later defended her role in the sex-motivated slayings by testifying that Gallego intimidated her with violence and mental control. "Everything I would make, my payroll check, had to be turned over to Gerry."

The jurors and spectators alike were probably somewhat moved by Charlene's testimony, which was generally poised and articulate. The prosecution had faced a real dilemma, since its most critical witness was also a confessed murderess and co-conspirator in the crimes in which she was testifying against her husband. How to present a believable, vulnerable, witness who was also a victim was tricky since the jury might have also seen

Charlene as a conniving, treacherous, two-timing killer out to save her own pretty neck at the expense of her one-time, co-defendant husband.

By most accounts, Charlene held up very well under direct examination. Only once did she break down in tears—when asked to identify a photo of Mary Beth Sowers. Pound for pound of her small frame, Charlene looked for all the world like every word she uttered was the truth and nothing but the truth so help her.

Of course, Charlene was used to being convincing when she had to be. She had convinced Detective Trujillo twice. She had also convinced Detectives Taylor and Burchett that she was telling the truth. In each instance she had, in fact, lied.

Now Charlene faced her biggest challenge, the one every person in the courtroom had waited for. It was Gerald Gallego's turn to cross-examine the witness.

TWENTY-THREE

Gerald Armond Gallego opened the cross-examination of his wife, Charlene, on Tuesday, January 11, 1983, more than two years after the couple was arrested in Omaha and charged with the kidnapping and murders of Craig Miller and Mary Beth Sowers. Since then, Charlene had agreed to turn State's evidence in return for leniency. In the process, she betrayed the man she had married twice—the one who had spared her life.

Now he faced the fight of his own life, as a conviction would almost certainly mean the gas chamber. And he would have Charlene to thank for it.

The confrontation between Gallego and Charlene never quite materialized as had been expected on this first day of cross-examination. Attorney Gallego tried to present a picture of professionalism, and witness Charlene acted as if she was testifying before a real attorney in showing detachment from the man she had once loved and obeyed blindly.

Gallego got Charlene to admit that she had once confronted him with her chrome-plated .25 caliber pistol after he threatened to leave her for another woman. Charlene also admitted, under cross-examination, that she was free to leave Gallego at any time during their relationship.

At one point, Gerald sought to establish Charlene's admiration for him after they first met.

"You were pleasantly surprised because I did not force myself on you sexually, weren't you?"

"Yes," Charlene answered. "You conducted yourself as a gentleman that night."

"And the following morning, what was delivered to your front door?"

"A dozen long-stemmed roses with a card." She said it read: "To a very sweet girl. Gerry."

Gallego eventually got Charlene to admit that she had tried many drugs over the course of their relationship.

On the second day of Gallego's cross-examination of Charlene, things became more heated between the former husband and wife.

"Mrs. Gallego"—Gallego addressed Charlene as such throughout much of the trial—"I don't know if I've ever asked you this before. Did you kill Craig Miller?"

"No, I did not!" came her sharp response.

"Did you kill Mary Beth Sowers?"

"No, I did not."

"Have you ever killed anybody?"

"No, I have not."

"This incident is clear in your mind, isn't it?"

"Very."

"Has it always been clear in your mind?"

"Yes, it always will be." Charlene's voice quavered and tears rolled down her cheeks.

"Just answer the question, please," demanded Gallego, unmoved by her display of emotion.

This kind of fragmented, spontaneous questioning and response continued throughout the day.

Gallego appeared to become sentimental when he said to Charlene: "You know I love your mother. Wouldn't you agree that your mother has been more of a mother to me than my own mother?"

He added that he had not cross-examined Mercedes Williams, to his credit, he honestly believed.

"I'm sorry," said Charlene, "I don't understand you."

Gallego asked her bluntly: "Isn't it a fact Mrs. Williams is committing perjury for you?"

"I beg your pardon?"

Gallego asked Charlene to restate her testimony that he killed Miller and Sowers as part of a sexual fantasy.

221

"In brief," she said, "you wanted a young girl to take and keep for whatever you wanted."

Gallego now wanted Charlene to elaborate more on the notion of "the girl with heart" and "the competition for real love."

"Did I talk about this 'girl with heart' a lot?"

"Yes, you did."

"Okay. Who is she? Where's she from? What did she do? What did she do with so much heart that involved a sex fantasy that you would want to model yourself after her? Explain it to me . . ."

Charlene gave a long sigh. "To explain in detail, I would have to speak to my attorney."

Day three of Gerald Gallego's cross-examination of Charlene Gallego was marked by hostilities, cynicism, accusations and frustration from defense attorney Gallego and witness Charlene, once lovers, now combatants.

"I killed Craig Miller?" Gallego asked the witness mockingly.

"Yes, you did, Gerry!"

"How did I kill Craig Miller?"

"With a gun. You were standing face to face. You shot Craig Miller right there in front of the car," Charlene tearfully testified.

"Was he saying anything at the time?"

"I don't know," she stammered. "It didn't look like you gave him much chance."

This irritated Gallego and he said to the judge: "Your Honor, I would ask that the witness answer yes or no, then explain later."

The judge responded: "I think that question was answered."

Charlene testified that she saw three flashes of light when Craig Miller was falling down.

"So he was falling when three flashes of light went off?" Gallego repeated her account, even as Charlene openly wept.

"Gerry, for heaven's sake!"

Gallego yelled back: "If you don't think I'm going to fight for my life."

The judge broke in before things could get out of hand.

Later, Gallego asked Charlene if she was afraid after seeing the alleged killing of Craig Miller.

"I guess it was more of a shock," said the witness.

"Weren't you afraid after the shock or was it all a shock? What are your feelings at the time. You'd just seen me kill a man."

"Gerry, I've never seen anybody get killed before. How do you expect me to feel?"

Charlene testified that Mary Beth Sowers was forced to lay on the floorboards in the back seat of the Oldsmobile as she was being driven to the scene where she was to be killed.

Upon stopping, said Charlene to Gallego: "You asked me a question."

"What did I ask you?"

"You asked me if I wanted to kill her."

"What happened then?"

"I said, 'No, Gerry. You said I'd never have to do that.' Then you took her out of the car."

"Did I indicate: 'Hey, I'll be right back' or something like that? Did I indicate anything to you?"

"Just that you were taking her out to kill her."

Charlene Gallego's fifth day on the witness stand and fourth under cross-examination by defendant Gerald Gallego, acting as his own attorney, continued to fascinate spectators. This was no less true when Gallego got Charlene to admit to having a lesbian affair with an inmate at the Sacramento County women's detention facility near Elk Grove.

When asked to describe her relationship with the inmate, Charlene responded: "At one time we became very, very close and it was deemed as a homosexual affair."

The judge would not allow Gallego to pursue this line of questioning any further since the affair occurred well after the crimes in which Gallego was now on trial for and therefore was irrelevant to the proceedings.

Earlier Gallego had asked Charlene if she expected him to cover for her as the real murderer.

224

"No, Gerry," snapped Charlene, "I have never killed anybody in my life."

"I can prove that you have, Mrs. Gallego," Gallego countered, drawing a reprimand from the judge. The jury was instructed to disregard Gallego's remarks.

Often the drama played out between Gallego and Charlene resembled more of a lovers' spat than ex-lovers facing multiple murder charges.

Gallego asked Charlene if she had ever loved him.

"Yes," she admitted.

"What time was that?"

"It's been almost five years ago."

"So you haven't loved me since then?"

"Gerry, it was a love that turned into fear," cried Charlene. "Sometimes one outweighed the other."

"Well, did you love me at the time of our arrest?" asked Gallego.

"No, it was more of a protection. You kept telling me over and over how much you loved me and how much you would take care of me and never let anybody hurt me." She paused and added dismissively: "Which was another lie."

Smarting, Gallego noted: "You're no longer under my influence or my control or whatever."

"No, Gerry," Charlene begged to differ, "I've been under your control even after being arrested, up until the time when you said, 'Stay in love and you'll stay alive.' " She testified that Gallego issued this ominous warning to her shortly after their arrest in November 1980.

Just before adjournment, Gallego produced a Thanksgiving card that Charlene had sent to him in 1981 after she had been unsuccessful in an earlier attempt to plea bargain by testifying against Gallego. He passed the card to the clerk who then handed it to the judge and requested that Charlene read it aloud.

Charlene did, with several emotional breaks in between:

> "Happy Thanksgiving and may God be with you.
>
> Dear Gerry,
>
> I know it's been a long time, but with it being Thanksgiving time, I've been thinking of all I have to be thankful for and everything that God has blessed me with. A beautiful son, a loving family, and four years of the most beautiful memories in my life.
>
> I love you. I always have and always will. I don't know if I'm supposed to and I know nobody likes it, but I want to write to you.
>
> I miss you so very much and I love you with all my heart.
>
> I'm tired of playing all these games and through

*the Lord, I have learned right and wrong, love and
faith, and to count my blessings.*

> *All my love.*
> *Your punkin.*
> *Charlene."*

The card was dated November 22, 1981; exactly
one year to the day after the decomposed remains
of Mary Beth Sowers were found in a shallow pasture in Placer County. Charlene's own words probably said as much about her true nature as the man
to whom she sent the card.

Day five of Gallego's cross-examination of Charlene drew repeated reprimands from Judge Norman Spellberg for making improper asides.

"Isn't it a fact . . . you are a murderess?" Gallego
spat at Charlene.

"No, I am not, Gerry!" she returned hotly.

"Yes, you are!"

"You liar!"

The judge intervened in what sounded like two
children arguing frivolously.

Gallego went to great lengths to try and show
Charlene to be a liar and murderess who would
say anything to escape the gas chamber.

"You are willing to fabricate damaging testimony in order to sell your story?" argued Gallego.

"No," came a blunt response.

"It really doesn't bother you to fabricate evidence, does it? Whether 1981 or 1982 or 1983?"

"Yes, Mr. Gallego, it does."

Charlene testified that she and Gallego began fabricating stories after their arrest in Omaha.

"You knew you had something to cover up," she said to Gallego.

"Mrs. Gallego, the only one who seems to be covering up is you."

"Gerry, you know very well that you shot and killed those two kids."

Gallego continued to try and pin at least one of the murders on Charlene. He asked her if she took him to Placer County to show where she shot Mary Beth Sowers.

Charlene retorted angrily: "Gerry, I did not shoot and kill Mary Beth Sowers and you, of all people, should know that!"

Gallego's sixth and final day of cross-examination of his—as far as he was concerned—wife, Charlene, followed much of the same pattern of the previous days. He was able to cause the prosecution's star witness to quaver here and there but was unable to break her completely. Charlene held her ground on the kidnap and murders of Craig Miller and Mary Beth Sowers in which she pointed the finger directly at Gerald Gallego.

Gallego had lost any power over Charlene he had once possessed. But he was a desperate man and an incompetent attorney. That unstable combination allowed him to press on and hope for a miracle.

"Do you think if you had told the prosecutor that you shot and killed Mary Beth Sowers the judge would have made a deal with you?" Gallego asked Charlene.

"That is not the case."

"That's not a bad deal, is it? Wouldn't you agree that the deal you made is a lot better than standing trial and facing the possibility of conviction and the death penalty?"

"In some respects, yes. But in one aspect, no."

Gallego did not ask her to clarify that one aspect.

"Isn't it true that this deal was made with the district attorney of Sacramento County on the premise that you actually never killed anyone?"

"Yes."

"Isn't it true that after numerous attempts to make a deal on various stories you finally connected?"

"I cannot agree to the way you put it," said Charlene.

"Well, you understand what I'm saying, don't you?"

"If I did, I would have given you a straight answer."

"Mrs. Gallego, isn't the bottom line of your deal to blame both these murders on me to save yourself?"

"No it is not!" responded the witness tartly.

TWENTY-FOUR

Having failed to convince anyone that Charlene's testimony against him was false, Gerald Gallego did what any capable attorney would have probably advised him not to do. He put himself on the stand.

The prosecution could not have asked for a better witness to nail down the conviction. Gallego's contradictions, inconsistencies, arrogance, and unpreparedness as a witness in his own defense all proved to be his undoing, especially when coupled with the physical evidence and the strong, convincing testimony of Charlene Gallego.

Apparently Gallego recognized the error of his legal ways. In his closing arguments, the attorney-defendant conceded that he had taken a "legal licking" in the trial. Yet he insisted that he told the truth about the deaths of Craig Miller and Mary Beth Sowers and asked the jury to "believe me on faith, if nothing else . . ."

Gallego admitted once more, to those who could sentence him to death, that he shot and killed Craig Miller, adding: "I had no intent to kill Craig Miller and, most of all, I had no premeditation and I had no deliberation."

Gallego insisted that it was Charlene who shot and killed Mary Beth Sowers.

"I did not kill Mary Beth Sowers," said Gallego. "I did not aid, abet, command, console, contribute and whatever goes with that, and I would ask that you believe me . . . I didn't do it."

He again pitted the truthfulness of his testimony against that of Charlene's. ". . . This whole case returns to her [Charlene Gallego] and I ask you not to believe her. I ask you to believe me."

In referring to the alleged "sexual fantasies" that Charlene testified were the motivating factor for the kidnap-slayings, Gallego dismissed it as a big lie, using words unseemly for an attorney hoping to convince a jury.

"I can honestly tell you," he claimed, "I'm not bragging, but if I've had problems with girls, it's not because I haven't had enough. It's because I had too many."

Near the end of his presentation, Gallego appeared to show some compassion for the woman he had married twice and who had ultimately betrayed him.

"I'm not mad at Charlene for making this deal. I don't like the way she did it. I don't like the stories she told, but I don't want her hurt. As much as I dislike it, she still has my son."

In fact, it would be a very long time before Charlene would ever have her son.

In closing, Gerald Gallego threw himself at the mercy of the jury to "give me the benefit of the doubt that I'm entitled to under the law. Look at the evidence, then decide for yourself."

During the trial, Gallego's mother, Lorraine Davies, had also appealed to the jury in deciding her son's fate. Testifying via a taped sworn statement, Lorraine Davies blamed Gallego's criminal behavior on a childhood fraught with neglect, abandonment, mental and physical abuse.

Then there was his daddy, Gerald Albert Gallego, himself a multiple murderer, who was executed in Mississippi's gas chamber in 1955. Since Gallego never met his father, Davies placed more blame for her son's life on one of his stepfathers prior to her marriage to Ed Davies. The stepfather was alleged to be an alcoholic, wife beater, and child abuser.

If these mitigating factors were given any weight during the jury deliberations, it likely was not enough to affect the outcome of the verdict. All criminals tend to have some background circumstances that, in the minds of some people, seem to justify aberrant behavior. But a jury in a criminal trial is less concerned with predisposition and social-psychological profiles and backgrounds than the evidence against the accused. For Gerald Gallego, this was not good news.

The jury was given twenty-four options in deciding the guilt or innocence of Gerald Gallego. These included sixteen possible verdicts on the murder charges and eight possible findings on the kidnapping counts. In addition to Gallego's guilt or innocence, the jury would also have to decide if special circumstances were present during the alleged crimes "the commission of multiple murder, and murder during commission of kidnapping." If special circumstances were found to apply, then Gallego could be sentenced to death in California's gas chamber.

While the jury deliberated, Gerald Gallego sat in a holding cell reading, *Tarnsman of Gor*, a book by author John Norman, who also wrote *Slave Girl of Gor* and *Imaginative Sex*. "Gor" is described in the book as "a world of slaves and beautiful women, of human domination by the alien, secret Priest-Kings," and "the world of Talena, tempestuous daughter of the greatest warlord of Gor. She waited for the man who could subdue her—the man who would be her master."

On the front cover of *Tarnsman of Gor* is a beautiful woman, unclothed and kneeling at the feet of her sword-wielding master. There is a chain around her neck and her arms are bound behind her back.

Perhaps Gallego viewed himself as such a master and his murdered victims as his slaves? Or maybe, in his desperation to escape a sure fate, Gallego hoped he might somehow be transported to this fictional world of sex slaves and masters? It would not happen—at least not before the verdict came in.

On June 21, 1983, Gerald Armond Gallego was sentenced to death for the November 2, 1980, kidnapping-murders of college sweethearts Craig Miller and Mary Beth Sowers.

It took the jury less than two hours of deliberations and only one ballot to decide that Gallego was to have a date with California's gas chamber . . . at least in theory.

Mary Beth Sowers's grandmother applauded the sentence and seemed to reflect the feelings of all the families of the victims when she said: "I don't think we could have stood it if it had been anything besides the death penalty."

The six-month trial of Gerald Gallego did not

come cheaply for the taxpayers of California, costing more than a million dollars.

Few would argue that the money was not well spent, considering the heinous crimes Gerald Gallego had committed in the state, two of which he was now convicted of.

Mary Beth and Craig would finally be able to rest a little easier. California's other victims, Virginia Mochel, Kippi Vaught, and Rhonda Scheffler, would not have their day in court. However, the verdict represented a victory for them, as well as Gallego's other victims.

For many, the only true justice would be when and if Gallego's death sentence was carried out. This appeared to be a long shot at best in California, where the last execution had taken place in 1967. California State Supreme Chief Justice Rose Bird was a staunch opponent of the death penalty. Indeed, the liberal California Supreme Court had reversed eighteen of twenty-one death penalty verdicts—many as the result of minor technicalities. Under the circumstances, few were optimistic that Gerald Gallego would ever come face to face with California's gas chamber. It would certainly come no sooner than the 133 others waiting on death row at the time.

In this instance, justice had an ace in the hole or a second chance. The state of Nevada was fully prepared to try Gerald Gallego on four counts of murder. The death penalty was generally thought to have a much better chance to be carried out in Nevada due to less complicated pretrial motions, tougher rules, and a far more conservative State Supreme Court than its neighbor. Pershing County District Attorney Richard Wagner had waited impatiently for the California trial to end so that the Nevada trial could begin.

For Gerald and Charlene Gallego, they were only halfway through the legal process. For the families of their victims, the nightmare continued.

TWENTY-FIVE

Following the California trial, Gerald and Charlene Gallego engaged in legal Ping-Pong with the states of California and Nevada, as the convicted murderer and confessed murderess each fought individual battles to keep their opponents at bay. Both Gallegos would ultimately spend years in the Nevada correctional system, but not before a number of challenges threatened to undo things.

In November 1983, Charlene Gallego's negotiated plea bargain nearly came apart when the California Board of Prison Terms refused to guarantee a prison term of sixteen years, eight months for the first-degree murders of Craig Miller and Mary Beth Sowers. Ultimately, a Sacramento County Supeior Court judge dropped the California charges against Charlene. Still intact was the Nevada side

R. BARRI FLOWERS

of the plea bargain, which also called for a sixteen
year, eight month sentence for the second-degree
murders of seventeen-year-olds, Karen Chipman
Twiggs and Stacy Redican.

Meanwhile, Gerald Gallego was battling the system for his very life. The state of Nevada had
moved swiftly to extradite Gallego following his
June 1983 sentence of death in a Martinez, California courtroom. However, Gallego, aware that execution was more likely in Nevada with its
conservative Supreme Court, was in no hurry to
die. He fought extradition through the legal system. In September 1983, California's Governor
George Deukmejian ordered the "prompt" extradition of Gallego to Nevada. An executive agreement signed by Nevada's Governor Richard Bryan
all but assured that if found guilty of the charges
of kidnapping, rape, and murder, Gallego would
remain in Nevada until his execution was carried
out or he was successful in appealing his death sentence. Should the latter occur, Gallego would be
returned to California's death row.

Gallego managed to delay the inevitable by several months. A request by Gallego's attorney for a
writ of *habeas corpus* and an extended delay of the
extradition process, pending the automatic Supreme Court appeal of Gallego's California death
sentence, was denied by an appeals court on January 10, 1984. This followed a December 1983 order

240

by a Marin County judge for Gallego to be extradited to Nevada.

Before Gallego could get a ruling from the California Supreme Court in a last minute attempt to halt the extradition, he was hurriedly picked up at San Quentin prison by members of the Sacramento County Sheriff's Department, driven to Sacramento, and flown to Reno on a sheriff's department Air Squadron plane. From Reno, Gallego was driven ninety-two miles to Lovelock, Nevada where he was to be put on trial.

The California Supreme Court refused to block Gallego's extradition.

Less than twenty-four hours after Gerald Gallego was transferred from San Quentin's death row to Pershing County, Nevada, he was formally charged with the murders of Stacy Redican, Karen Chipman Twiggs, Brenda Judd, and Sandra Colley. Gallego was also charged with four counts of kidnapping and four counts of rape. He was represented by Nevada State Public Defender Tom Perkins.

The accused was dressed in jeans and a sweatshirt, as he glared at spectators while standing before Justice of the Peace Gordon Richardson. This glare of contempt was to typify Gallego's disposition throughout the Nevada proceedings against him.

The pretrial process carried on into February 1984, with Charlene taking her turn in the spotlight. At issue again was the legality of Charlene's marriages to Gerald Gallego. Under Nevada law, she could be prevented from testifying against Gallego pertaining to certain communications between them as husband and wife, had either of their marriages proven to be valid.

Justice of the Peace James Mancuso ruled that Charlene was never legally married to Gerald Gallego and thereby could testify fully against him with her allegations that he murdered ten people, four of them in Nevada. The decision was based on Nevada investigators producing evidence that Gallego had not legally divorced at least one of five wives to precede Charlene.

At the hearing, Charlene was allowed to see her son, Gerald A. Gallego, Jr., who was now three. He had been accompanied to the Pershing County Courthouse by Charlene's parents, Charles and Mercedes Williams.

At the close of the three-day preliminary hearing, Mancuso ruled that there was sufficient evidence to believe that Gallego kidnapped and murdered the four girls, while dismissing the four counts of sexual assault for lack of evidence. Gallego was bound over to district court for trial.

During the hearing, Gallego attempted to discharge his attorneys, Tom Perkins and Gary Marr,

and take over his own defense as he had unsuccessfully done in California. The judge denied his
request and ordered that Perkins and Marr continue as his attorneys.

District Attorney Richard Wagner and Sheriff
James McIntosh of Pershing County wanted nothing more than to see Gerald Gallego convicted for
the kidnapping-murders of Sacramentans Stacy
Ann Redican and Karen Chipman Twiggs, and
Nevadans Brenda Lynne Judd and Sandra Kay
Colley. This was made possible by the confession
of Charlene Gallego and her implication of Gerald
Gallego as the girls' killer. Charlene's testimony
and memory of the murders for investigators to follow would make or break the case against Gallego.

By far the strongest case was made for Gallego's
abduction and murder of Redican and Twiggs. For
one, the authorities had bodies to corroborate Charlene's story. A key piece of physical evidence came
when Charlene led investigators to her parents'
house and pointed out a ball of white macrame
rope that was in the trunk of Gallego's Triumph.
Charlene identified the rope as the material used
to bind Twiggs and Redican. The rope was ultimately traced to a Sacramento store.

A criminalist, Allan Gilmore, compared samples
of the macrame found in Gallego's car with the material binding the hands of Redican and Twiggs.

Gilmore found that it was of the same type, composition, diameter, and color. In other words, the two materials were one and the same.

Charlene told investigators that she cut the rope under Gallego's orders and he used it to tie the victims' hands before murdering them.

Unfortunately, Charlene's assistance in gathering evidence in the Judd-Colley kidnapping-murders proved less successful. Although Charlene led investigators on a search for the burial site of the victims in an area northeast of Lovelock, she was unable to pinpoint exactly where the teenagers were bludgeoned to death. Nor did the removal of earth in and around the vicinity turn up a clue.

The bodies of Brenda Lynne Judd and Sandra Kay Colley, fourteen and thirteen respectively, were never found. Without this crucial evidence that their murders had occurred, there was no case against Gallego.

The prosecution was now down to two murders for which to try Gerald Gallego.

Other unexpected problems surfaced along the way to trial. In late October 1983, a key prosecution witness died of cancer. The witness was to testify that he saw Gallego carrying a gun to the site where Stacy Redican and Karen Twiggs were found slain near Lovelock.

According to the witness, who was a miner, he

had been working at a mine over the hill around the time Twiggs and Redican were killed, when he saw a man he identified as Gerald Gallego with a gun in a strapped-on holster.

The prosecution considered the witness important to the case against Gallego because he gave a "very positive statement that he had seen Gallego there at the grove of trees where the bodies were recovered."

Another serious concern turned out to be the cost of the trial. It was estimated it would cost about $60,000—a fraction of the cost of Gallego's California trial—a sum representing nearly one-third of Pershing County's budget. Many of the 3,500 residents of sagebrush-covered Pershing County were outraged at the cost and not afraid to voice their displeasure over the county footing the bill for this trial. After all, Gallego had already been convicted of two murders and sentenced to death. How many times could a person die? And at what cost?

From the standpoint of Pershing County officials, they strongly felt the expense of trying Gallego was well worth it at any cost.

"Sixty thousand dollars is a significant amount for a small community," said D.A. Wagner. "But it is not an unbearable expense. There has been some opposition because of the cost, but I think a community must have enough pride to pay for this type of case. I think that we must say that we cannot tolerate this kind of behavior, that we refuse to let our community be used as a graveyard and dumping ground for such atrocious crimes."

The greater motivation for Pershing County's district attorney was the fear that Gallego would never be put to death in California, but stood a good chance to be executed in Nevada where only twenty inmates sat on death row at the time. (The last Nevada execution had taken place in October 1979, when Jesse Walter Bishop was sent to the gas chamber in Carson City for killing a man during a robbery. California's last execution had been carried out in April 1967, when Aaron Mitchell died in San Quentin's gas chamber for killing a police officer.)

Wagner reflected this feeling when he complained about California's "liberal court attitudes" as compelling reasons to put Gallego on trial in Nevada: "You [Californians] still have Sirhan Sirhan in prison down there; there's even talk of turning him loose . . . California's judicial climate is so liberal, I'd hate to predict how Gallego's case will end up there." (As of this writing, California has resumed its execution of death row inmates, with two being put to death between 1992 and 1993.)

Fortunately, Pershing County would not have to bear the cost of the trial alone. After a *Sacramento Bee* columnist wrote about the financial burden the county faced to try Gallego, donations began to pour in from throughout the country, led by California.

"Hang him high!" said one note attached to a ten dollar bill. "Good luck in hanging Gallego," said an Idaho man in sending fifty dollars, "hope Charlene is next!" An East Coast woman sent twenty dollars and told why in a note: "I have a daughter about the same age as the victims. I want to know that [Gallego] will not live to kill again."

The donations ranged from well-worn dollar bills to corporate checks of one hundred dollars. In all, nearly $28,000 was raised to help defray the cost of the trial.

"It is absolutely beautiful," said the Pershing County clerk-treasurer. "I've never seen anything like this."

The message seemed to be loud and clear. Citizens were fed up with violent crime and violent criminals not being held accountable sufficient to the crime or crimes they committed.

With nearly half the trial paid for up front, the People were as prepared as they ever would be to take on Gerald Gallego.

TWENTY-SIX

Gerald Armond Gallego went on trial for the second time on May 23, 1984, for the kidnapping and murders of Karen Chipman Twiggs and Stacy Ann Redican.

Outside the Pershing County Courthouse, amidst green elm trees, stood a granite monument with the Ten Commandments inscribed on it. Inside sat a serial murderer who had probably broken every one of them at some time or another in his thirty-seven plus years.

The courtroom where Gerald Gallego's guilt or innocence would be decided was built in 1920, round, and under a silver dome. On the bench was Judge Llewellyn A. Young and in the jury box were six women and six men who could sentence Gallego to death.

District Attorney Richard Wagner—a devout Mormon, husband, and father of seven—pulled no punches in outlining the case against Gallego during his opening statement.

"He planned to kidnap young girls to use for his sexual pleasure," Wagner told the jury. He then told them how Gallego had stopped at a Reno store to purchase a hammer, drove to an isolated area some twenty miles outside of Lovelock, and bludgeoned to death Twiggs and Redican, whom he had kidnapped at gunpoint.

Wagner did not go lightly on his key witness, Charlene Gallego, acknowledging to the jury that as an accomplice to the killings the jury should be "leery" of her. But he added: "I will bring to you other evidence that will show she is not lying."

Gallego's attorney, Deputy Public Defender Gary Marr, was more forceful in his depiction of Charlene as the prosecution's star witness in his opening statement.

"Charlene Gallego made a plea bargain in this case," Marr emphasized to the jury. "She testifies against Gerald Gallego—she lies and escapes the death penalty."

Marr went on to refer to Charlene as a "confessed murderess" who has "told different stories at different times ... We're going after her. We want you to get a look at what Charlene Gallego is really like ... We're not apologizing for the defendant. We're going all out. We're going to the wall for this man."

Gallego would need all the help he could get from his attorneys.

Charlene Williams, as she now referred to herself, took the stand for the first time on the second day of the trial. Under direct examination, she testified that her steady relationship with Gallego fell somewhere between love, desperation, and being on the rebound from two failed marriages.

"The only reason for . . . being with Gerry wasn't just love," claimed Charlene, "it was needing someone. He was security. I didn't want to fail again."

The witness told the jury of her impressions of the accused when they first met in September 1977.

"I thought he was a very nice, clean-cut fellow," said Charlene. Then: "Gerry changed . . . At first he was considerate, polite and fun to be with. Then he became domineering. I was supposed to do what I was told."

Charlene later discussed their sex life. "If there was a problem in the bedroom, it was my fault . . . he was having a problem reaching—ummm . . ."

"Sexual climax?"

"Yes. He tried different types of sex, but it was always my fault—I was doing something wrong.

He wanted a certain type of sex. If I said that it
hurt, that was too bad."

Charlene moved on to Gallego's sex fantasies.
"He had this fantasy about having girls that would
be there whenever he wanted them and do whatever he wanted them for. He said he wanted young
girls ripe for picking."

All the while, Gallego sat at the defense table
staring stonefaced at Charlene while twirling his
pen atop a yellow legal pad, almost as if it was his
one-time partner in crime.

In attempting to show a "common scheme" in
Gallego's killing spree, prosecutor Wagner had
Charlene testify about Gallego's murder of his first
two victims, Kippi Vaught and Rhonda Scheffler.

"[Gallego] told me to turn the radio up all the
way and not to turn around," wept Charlene. "I
heard what I thought were pops. Gerry came back
and told me to move over and got into the driver's
seat. Then Gerry said one of the girls was still wig-
gling and he got back out and he shot her again."

Gallego's Public Defender, Tom Perkins, got his
chance to cross-examine Charlene the following
day. He did his best to try and portray Charlene as
cold, clever, and manipulative.

"You learned how to get things you wanted by
acting hurt, by crying and acting like a child, by

humiliating the person, right?" Charlene was asked sharply by Perkins.

The witness denied it.

When it was suggested straightforwardly that Charlene lied about Gallego to escape the death penalty, she responded: "I lied for love, not life."

"When the relationship wasn't working, you knew how to get out of it, didn't you?"

"Yes, but I think it needs an explanation."

The defense did not allow Charlene to elaborate.

"You liked that lifestyle. You wanted to be with Gerald, didn't you?"

"Yes," Charlene admitted.

Perkins asked the witness if she said to Gallego after he killed his first victims: " 'I'm glad you did it because I thought I was going to have to.' "

"Yes," came a hesitant response.

"The lies you told were designed to protect Gerald, is that what you want us to believe?"

She said yes.

"The truth is you were trying to protect yourself . . . right?"

Charlene vehemently denied this.

When questioned earlier by the prosecutor, Charlene had said she had been completely truthful during the trial.

The next time Charlene took the stand, she told the jury how she and Gallego lured Stacy Redican and Karen Twiggs to their kidnapping and deaths.

"Gerry pointed out two girls. I walked up to them. I told them that we were talking about marijuana. I said something about a party; referring to marijuana."

After driving the girls to Limerick Canyon, testified Charlene, "Gerry came out of the van and called me over. He asked me if I wanted these girls. I told him no."

Later, Charlene told the jury that Gallego led her to the graves where he had buried Stacy and Karen.

"He told me, 'Don't worry about it, they're already dead.' He had a piece of broken branch . . . he was smoothing the ground."

Under direct examination a day later, Charlene, frequently sobbing, told the jury she deserved to be executed for her role in the murders of Twiggs and Redican.

"I have nothing to save my life for. No matter what I do, there is nothing that will ever bring those children back."

"Have I or anyone else in law enforcement ever indicated that we think you deserve anything less [than the death penalty]?" asked the prosecutor.

"No, Mr. Wagner," sobbed the witness.

Later Charlene testified: "It was my duty, my responsibility to please [Gallego], to be what he wanted me to be. I was to accept him . . . to accept my role. I knew I would never find anyone else who wanted me. I was afraid of him at the time. I was afraid that he would kill me. The only way he could end this relationship was to kill me because of what I knew."

In Gallego's first trial, Charlene testified that she was free to leave Gallego any time she wanted.

Charlene went on to tell the jury that the day Gallego murdered Redican and Twiggs, he told her [Charlene] she was "stupid and unattractive... Gerry used that day to prove to me who was boss, who was in control, and who was nothing."

Gallego's defense attorney sought to undermine Charlene's credibility at every chance, while Gallego himself maintained a speechless scowl throughout the trial.

"A lot of the things you've come up with over time are things that make Gerald look worse, aren't they?" Perkins asked.

Charlene tearfully denied this.

"Your memory about things that make Gerald look bad is better today than two years ago, right?"

Again the witness begged to differ.

Perkins, annoyed at the sobbing Charlene had become particularly adept at, asked her tonelessly: "You know that if you cry maybe a strong man will leave you alone, don't you?"

The witness was speechless for a moment or two before denying it.

* * *

It took the six man, six woman jury just two and a half hours of deliberation before condemning Gerald Armond Gallego to death by lethal injection for the murders of Karen Chipman Twiggs and Stacy Ann Redican. Almost for effect, the jury also convicted the serial killer of two counts of kidnapping, and sentenced him to consecutive life terms in state prison without the possibility of parole. Upon hearing the verdict, Gallego squeezed his eyes shut, then returned to that blank stare at the table before him.

Family members of the victims could hardly contain their delight at the just sentence of death for Gallego and the realization that their ordeal was just about over.

"We can go on with our lives now," expressed Stacy Redican's mother. "I have three other children and we've put a lot of this behind us. It's been a healing process over the years. We'll just keep on with it."

In spite of the fact that Brenda Judd and Sandra Colley's bodies were never found, their parents were no less pleased with the verdict against the man who was implicated in their deaths.

"Now it's time for my family to rebuild," said Brenda's mother. "It helps me to know that this man is going to pay whether my daughter's name was mentioned on that stand or not. He's paying for all the deeds that he did. Not just for the ones mentioned in court."

These sentiments were echoed by Sandra's mother. "Justice was served today," she stated. "The sucker deserves what he got."

Most present seemed in complete agreement.

At Gallego's formal sentencing on June 25, 1984, the twice-convicted multiple murderer and death row inmate lambasted those who tried and sentenced him. He profanely denied killing Twiggs and Redican and called the entire proceeding a travesty based on the testimony of one witness—his twice illegally married wife, Charlene—whom Gallego insisted fabricated her tale to save her own life.

"What you people done to me is wrong!" spat Gallego defiantly to the court, media, and anyone else present who cared to listen. In the process he had broken a stone-faced silence that had lasted throughout his trial. "You sentenced me to death with no damned evidence at all. I didn't kill those girls and you don't have a damned thing that says I did!"

Directing his rage at District Judge Llewellyn A. Young, Gallego had earlier questioned the fairness of his trial. "I was guilty before I got here, judge," he contended vehemently. "I was found guilty and sentenced long before the trial and anybody who

can't see that is a fool . . ." Glaring at prosecutor
Wagner, Gallego blared: "The only evidence he
brought against me was his hired gun"—referring
to once-upon-a-time wife turned State's chief witness, Charlene—"his paid assassin."

Wagner took umbrage to the suggestion that the
trial was anything but fair, insisting that Gallego
had been tried and found guilty "by a fair jury of
the people" and that the verdicts were strictly "in
line with the evidence."

But the prosecutor was not willing to leave it at
that. Triumphant in victory, he seemed personally
insulted that the gutless Gallego was trying to cast
a shadow on his conviction and death sentence.

In noting that Gallego's father had been executed
in Mississippi's gas chamber after being convicted
of two heinous murders, Wagner told the court, or
more specifically Gerald Gallego, that while the elder Gallego "died for what he did, at least he was
man enough to stand up and admit it . . . That
hasn't happened here."

Nor did it seem likely to, as Gallego favored the
prosecutor severely.

"I guess the worst part of it all," continued Wagner unaffectedly, "is that everyone keeps hoping
that maybe there's a little bit of humanity . . . just a
little bit of something worth saving. But it hasn't
been shown. Not even today. That great macho im-
age hasn't been man enough to acknowledge it."

Huffing and puffing mad, Gallego responded to the judge: "I don't know how the district attorney can say that, Your Honor." Once again Gallego faced the prosecutor that had adeptly spearheaded his second death sentence in a year. "Were you there?" he challenged Wagner in a voice that was without remorse. "The only thing you know is what Charlene Gallego told you, and the only thing she told you is what she wanted you to know."

Judge Young formally sentenced Gerald Gallego to death by lethal injection.

In the process, Gerald Armond Gallego got the distinction of being one of the few people in this country to be put on the death row of two states simultaneously. Some might say this was an unnecessary waste of taxpayer money and bureaucratic red tape, but for the families and friends of his victims it was a relatively small price to be paid for the lives Gerald Gallego took.

Although justice would never be fully served for Virginia Mochel, Linda Aguilar, Kippi Vaught, Rhonda Martin Scheffler, Brenda Judd, and Sandra Colley—whose abductions and murders Gerald Gallego was never put on trial for—testimony and evidence given at two other trials clearly connected Gallego to their deaths.

These victims could fully join hands with Craig Miller, Mary Beth Sowers, Stacy Ann Redican, and Karen Chipman Twiggs in being forever bound by fate and tragedy. All could be at peace in knowing that their killer would never again be free to deprive others of life and a future.

As of October 1994, Gerald Armond Gallego continues to sit on death row in the Nevada State Penitentiary in Carson City, Nevada. Sixteen years after he raped and murdered Rhonda Scheffler and Kippi Vaught and more than ten years after he was sentenced to death by lethal injection for the kidnap-murders of Stacy Redican and Karen Twiggs, Gerald Gallego has managed to hang on to his own life almost defiantly to the bitter end for those waiting for justice to be completed. Fortunately the appeals process has gone just about as far as it can for the serial rapist-killer. The U.S. Supreme Court is almost certain to reject his plea for leniency.

Gallego's date with destiny cannot be that far away. In the meantime, he has suffered from the loss of freedom and the prolonged distress of impending death. This should give some solace to those who wish justice had been a bit swifter.

As for Charlene Adell Williams, the former "Mrs. Gerald Gallego," she is serving out her plea-bargained time at the Department of Prisons Women's Center in Carson City, Nevada. She is due to be released in August 1997.

TWENTY-SEVEN

One subject that criminologists have long debated is the possibility that genes may somehow predispose one to criminal behavior. That is, criminals are the unfortunate result of genetic transmission of physical or mental abnormalities passed from one generation to another. For those who subscribe to this "bad seed" school of thought, Gerald Armond Gallego represents the quintessential case study. Gallego, currently on death row in two states for four murders, is the progeny of Gerald Albert Gallego. The elder Gallego also happened to be a multiple murderer who was put to death in Mississippi's new gas chamber when his son was still in grade school.

Does this mean that Gerald Armond Gallego is a chip off the psychopathic block? Did his father's violent tendencies get passed on to him and, in effect, guarantee that he too would someday become a murderer? Were that true, would Gallego therefore be "truly" responsible for crimes he was "born" to commit?

It does provide for fascinating speculation, given the bizarre and violent similarities between father and son. On the surface, such commonly used phrases as "like father, like son," "the black sheep of the family," and "bad blood" seem tailor-made for Gerald Gallego.

Researchers have in fact shown a relationship between heredity and generational patterns of criminal behavior. Two of the more interesting studies were done by Henry Goddard and Richard Dugale, who documented long histories of social aberrations such as "prostitution, idiocy, feeblemindedness, fornication, and delinquency" within certain families. Indeed, Gallego's own family tree appears to be fraught with abnormal behavior that extends well beyond his father.

This notwithstanding, few modern criminologists can take the notion of genetic predisposition to antisocial behavior seriously. Most research in this area tends to be heavily flawed and methodologically unsound, while failing to adequately account for free will and one's environment in the commission of crimes.

Certainly not all serial killers have killers for fathers any more than all rapists have rapists for fathers. In fact, Gerald Gallego's own mother committed suicide. Albeit this occurred years after Gallego was put on death row, the fact that he has his mother's genes as much as his father's would suggest (if genetic transmission of behavior were possible) that Gallego himself was also destined to commit suicide. That is, if his impending execution did not take place first. There is no reliable evidence that could support the possibility of genetically acquired behavioral abnormalities.

A much greater "predictor" of Gerald Gallego's violent criminal behavior can be found in his social and physical environment over the years. Gallego's education in crime probably occurred during his frequent time spent in juvenile detention and adult prisons. Much of his early scrapes with the law involved his half-brother, David Hunt, who had a different father than Gallego.

Ironically, Gallego's stepfathers may have had a much greater influence on his aberrant behavior than his real father, whom he never knew. According to Gallego's mother, Lorraine Davies, Gallego had at least one abusive and alcoholic stepfather.

Studies have shown a correlation between alcoholic and physically abusive parents and delinquency in children and future adult criminal behavior.

Although research continues on the role heredity

plays in our behavior, the relative weight of genetic and environmental influences on violent crime and criminals will likely always favor the social environment as having the stronger impact on criminal behavior.

Where does Gerald Gallego's free will fit into his sex-motivated murderous ways? Each of us must ultimately be held accountable for our own actions. Gallego is no exception. He is the classic sociopathic personality. This is a man who is mentally unstable, amoral, antisocial, egocentric, hostile, insensitive, and callous. He lacks normal feelings of obligation to conform to social norms and is without moral constraints. In other words, Gallego is probably one of the best examples of a person who has no real sense of social values and no regard for human life—except his own.

Would Gallego have killed had he not had his partner in crime and wife, Charlene, by his side? Most likely, yes. Indeed, who is to say that Gallego has not killed independently of Charlene? Many serial killers, once behind bars, have admitted that they killed far more people than the authorities ever knew about. Although Gallego has not made this claim, it certainly does not mean he was incapable or innocent of killing other women before and during his years with Charlene, apart from her.

The biggest mystery may be why Gallego did not kill Charlene, who ultimately proved to be his downfall. Whether it was love, need, attachment, underestimation or stupidity, he did the world a favor. Never again will Gerald Armond Gallego be in a position to handpick his victims, with or without his partner in murder and marriage.

As for Gerald's son, Gerald Armond Gallego, Jr., he may have his father's and grandfather's genes, but there is no reason to believe he will follow in their murderous footsteps. Of course, it remains to be seen how Gerald, Jr. will fare in life. The one thing we can be certain of is that he is not doomed from the start.

Meanwhile, Charlene Adell Williams, who sold out her husband to save her own life, will be out of prison in the summer of 1997. She will be a relatively young forty and free to live out her life without looking back.

How should this woman be judged? Was she a victim of fear, intimidation, and subjugation? Or was she more of a clever, selfish, heartless, drug-abusing manipulator who willingly helped her husband kidnap and murder ten people, one with child, before turning on Gallego when the going got tough?

We may never know the real answer, but the greater likelihood is that Charlene Williams is much closer to the latter than former portrayal. It is inconceivable that a woman with no criminal past, a high IQ and a well-to-do background could participate in the abduction and murder of at least eleven human beings and not come forward until she was apprehended. Yet this was the case for Charlene Williams, who never once alerted the police or even her doting parents as to what she and her husband, Gerald, were up to, even though she was free to come and go as she pleased for the most part and came in contact with authorities on more than one occasion.

We, in this society, like to believe that females nurture life more than take life away. Recent examples indicate that women can be serial killers as much as men. Most notably, in May 1992, Aileen Carol Wuornos, a thirty-six-year-old prostitute, was sentenced to Florida's electric chair for the first-degree murder of six of her customers. She was believed to have shot to death at least seven men over a twelve-month period.

Although Wuornos cold-bloodedly pulled the trigger on each of her victims, is she any more of a murderess than Charlene Williams, who confessed to four murders and admits to being an accomplice in seven others? In many respects, the way Charlene sweet and innocently lured most of her victims—young girls—to their deaths was far more vile and despicable than Wuornos's killing of adult male johns, many of whom she claimed were abusive to her. Charlene's victims never even had a chance once she delivered them into Gallego's sociopathic web.

While Aileen Wuornos has an almost certain date with the electric chair, incredibly, Charlene is within a few years of being released from prison after serving a plea-bargained term of only sixteen years, eight months for her active role in the murder of eleven people, including an unborn baby. How did Charlene manage to pull it off? The attorneys and investigators involved in the case will tell you that without her testimony against Gerald Gallego, he too might have walked after only a few years. True or not, it is hard to imagine that in October 1994—nearly twelve years after Charlene's plea bargain—such a cozy deal would be offered to a confessed serial killer of either sex.

To effect her deal, Charlene used her greatest gifts: a fragile appearance and uncanny ability to be convincing. These qualities served her well in luring her victims and conning investigators along the way into believing the stories she told them. This allowed the Gallegos' reign of terror to continue that much longer.

It is also likely that Charlene used her strengths to play on Gallego's weaknesses. Her intelligence was the perfect counter for his decidedly lower IQ. In Gallego's own way, he needed Charlene and she used that need to her own advantage. She knew she would not find another with whom she could share such a deadly secret life mixed in with drugs, alcohol, kinky sex and sex fantasies—all of which Charlene had to find as appealing in some respects as it was to Gerald Gallego, perhaps even addictive.

Only after the secret was out did Charlene abandon the man that she had so faithfully stood by for more than two brutal years. Like Gallego, Charlene is an interesting case study. She had every advantage in life, yet chose the likes of Gerald Gallego. What motivated her to embark on a life of violent crime with Gallego?

Fear? Submissiveness? Rebellion from her overly attentive parents? Rebound from disastrous earlier marriages? Gallego's machismo? Adventure? Substance abuse?

Perhaps all played an influential role; along with a weak and unbalanced personality characterized by feelings of jealousy, insecurity, helplessness, guiltlessness, impulsiveness, and immorality. Charlene Adell Williams cooperated with Gerald Gallego and his sex slave murders because she wanted to, not because she had to.

A final unnerving thought: Gerald and Charlene Gallego's story may not be atypical. Every year thousands of people are reported missing, thousands of others are found dead with readily available and pursued suspects—not all of which pan out. Given the relative ease, good fortune, and lack of detection that marked the Gallegos' twenty-six months of kidnapping, rape, and murder, it is highly possible that there are other couples, who are otherwise inconspicuous and suspicionless, perpetrating similar serial crimes.

It is likely that, as with the Gallegos, other male-female killing teams would only come to light after they have been apprehended. Until then, none of us can afford to be too careful or trusting . . .

ABOUT THE AUTHOR

R. Barri Flowers is a criminologist, novelist, and screenwriter. He is the author of ten books including *Women and Criminality* and the best-seller *The Adolescent Criminal*, as well as numerous articles and short stories. Mr. Flowers lives in Oregon with his wife.